D1093147

General Editors: J. R. MULRYNE
and J. C. BULMAN
Associate Editor: Margaret Shewring

Henry IV, Part One

Already published in the series

Volumes on most other plays in preparation

Of related interest

Henry IV, Part One

SCOTT McMILLIN

Manchester
University Press
Manchester and New York

Distributed exclusively in the USA and Canada by St. Martin's Press

Published by
Manchester University Press
Oxford Road, Manchester M13 9PL, UK
and Room 400, 175 Fifth Avenue,
New York, NY 10010, USA

Distributed exclusively in the USA and Canada
by St. Martin's Press, Inc.,175 Fifth Avenue,
New York, NY 10010, USA

British Library cataloguing in publication data
McMillin, Scott
    Henry IV, part one. – (Shakespeare in performance).
    1I. Title II Series
    822.3

Library of Congress cataloging in publication data
McMillin, Scott.
        Henry IV, part one / Scott McMillin.
        p. cm. -- (Shakespeare in performance)
        Includes bibliographical references and index.
        ISBN 0-7190-2729-2. -- ISBN 0-7190-2730-6 (pbk.)
        1. Shakespeare, William, 1564–1616. King Henry
        IV.
    2. Shakespeare, William, 1564–1616—Stage history. 3.
    Henry IV, King of England, 1367–1413, in fiction,
    drama, poetry, etc.
    I. Title. II. Title: Henry IV, part 1, III. Title: Henry the
    Fourth, part one. IV. Title: Henry the Fourth, part 1.
    V. Series.
    PR2810.M36 1991
    792.9'2—dc20   91-8716

ISBN 0 7190 2729 2 *hardback*
        0 7190 2730 6 *paperback*

Typeset by
Koinonia Limited, Manchester
Printed in Great Britain
by Bell & Bain Limited, Glasgow

CONTENTS

The illustrations appear between chapters II and III, pp. 34, 35

[v]

SERIES EDITORS' PREFACE

The study of Shakespeare's plays as scripts for performance in the theatre has grown in recent years to become a major interest for many university, college and secondary-school students and their teachers. The aim of the present series is to assist this study by describing how certain of Shakespeare's texts have been realised in production.

The series is not concerned to provide theatre histories. Rather, each contributor has selected a small number of productions of a particular play and studied them comparatively. The productions, often from different periods, countries and media, have been chosen because they are significant interpretations in their own right, but also because they represent something of the range and variety of possible interpretations of the play in hand. We hope that students and theatregoers, by reading these accounts of Shakespeare in performance, may enlarge their understanding of the text and begin, too, to appreciate some of the ways in which practical considerations influence the meanings a production incorporates: the stage the actor plays on, the acting company, the player's own physique and abilities, stage-design and theatre-tradition, as well as the political, social and economic conditions of performance and the expectations of a particular audience.

Any study of a Shakespeare text will reveal only a small proportion of the text's potential meaning. We hope that the effect of this series will be to encourage a kind of reading that is receptive to the ever-varying discoveries theatre interpretation provides.

J. R. Mulryne
J. C. Bulman
Margaret Shewring

ACKNOWLEDGEMENTS

Of those whom I wish to thank for helping me with this book, some work in theatres, some in libraries, some in both. Among the theatre people, I am glad to thank Sir Peter Hall, Stephanie Howard, Ian Judge, Ed Mirvish, Michael Pennington, Jen Stoller, and John Woodvine. The library people provided prompt-books and other material from the productions, along with encouragement and goodwill: Sylvia Morris, Marian Pringle, and Mary White of the Library at the Shakespeare Centre in Stratford, Christopher Robinson at the Theatre Collection of the University of Bristol, Sue Evans and Jane Morgan of the English Shakespeare Company, and Andrew Kirk of the London Theatre Museum. At several manuscript stages, James Bulman offered sympathetic critical readings which I found immensely valuable, and his fellow editors in the Shakespeare in Performance series, J. R. Mulryne and Margaret Shewring, each gave a meticulous and helpful review at a crucial point. Other colleagues and friends who responded to my pleas and queries with useful observations include Marvin Carlson, Alan Dessen, Barbara Hodgdon, Laurie Maguire, Michael Mullin, Richard Proudfoot, and Herbert Weil.

Some paragraphs from Chapter VI on the English Shakespeare Company first appeared in *Western European Stages* 2 (1990), pp. 57-60. For permission to reprint, I am grateful to the editor, Marvin Carlson. Quotations in Chapter VI from Lyons and Remy (eds.), *Chimes at Midnight, Orson Welles, director* are copyright 1988 Rutgers, The State University and are reprinted with permission of Rutgers University Press. Permission to reprint photographs has kindly been granted by the Shakespeare Birthplace Trust, Norma Campbell Vickers, Laurence Burns, and the Museum of Modern Art.

All references, unless otherwise noted, are to the Oxford edition of *Henry IV, Part One*, ed. David Bevington (Oxford, 1987).

CHAPTER I

Introduction

One decisive change marks the stage history of *1 Henry IV*, and it occurred in the twentieth century. What had been a 'Falstaff' play or, on occasion, a 'Hotspur' play – a play about one or both of the most flamboyant characters – came in the twentieth century to be seen as a study of political power with Prince Hal as the central character. That change of emphasis required a change of format. It takes both parts of *Henry IV* followed by *Henry V* to make Prince Hal into a fully-fledged hero, or anti-hero, and it was not until the mid-twentieth century that an influential cycle of these plays – influential enough to be imitated in later productions – was staged in the English theatre.

When it was first performed, in about 1596, *1 Henry IV* was immediately a Falstaff play. The fat knight was being quoted as though everyone knew his lines. 'Honour pricks them on,' says a letter of 1598 about a military venture of the day, 'and the world thinks that honour will quickly prick them off again' (Bevington, p. 2). In the same year, which is also the year the play was first published, the Earl of Essex made a joke about a friend's sister being married to Sir John Falstaff, and before long the Countess of Southampton was making an unkind remark about Falstaff being the father of someone's child (Hemingway, p. 446). No other Shakespearian character can be found circulating in social discourse so soon after appearing on the stage or in print.

Some of the early notoriety probably stemmed from the controversy over Falstaff's name (for he was originally meant to be Sir

John Oldcastle, a comic version of the famous Protestant martyr, and Shakespeare was apparently pressured to write in a new name), but the stage character was famous in his own right. The title page of the first edition does not mention Prince Hal and promises more of a battle 'between the King and Lord Henry Percy' than actually takes place at Shrewsbury, but with an eye for the trade it names the comic element accurately enough: 'With the humorous conceits of Sir John Falstaff.' Queen Elizabeth is said to have requested a play showing 'Sir John in love', and it is sometimes thought this is how *The Merry Wives of Windsor* came to be written. The existence of the rumour, not its veracity, illustrates the character's popularity. At the court of James I, the two *Henry IV* plays were sometimes known as 'Falstaff, Parts One and Two'.

Part One was one of the most popular Shakespeare plays after the Restoration, and the list of actors who played Falstaff and Hotspur includes almost every famous male performer in the history of the English-speaking theatre. To follow the more luminous names to 1900, Hotspur was undertaken by Thomas Betterton, Barton Booth, David Garrick (not successfully), J. P. and Charles Kemble, R. W. Elliston, William Macready, Edmund and Charles Kean, and Henry Wallack; Falstaff by William Cartwright, Betterton, James Quin, Stephen and Charles Kemble, Elliston, Samuel Phelps, James Hackett, and Beerbohm Tree. These are not generally regarded as good roles for women, but Ludia Webb played Falstaff in 1786 (*New York Times*, 29 June 1990 – which also reports on female Falstaffs in *The Merry Wives of Windsor*). So long as *Part One* is staged by itself, Falstaff ends at the peak of his renown, full of resiliency. For a moment it seems the fat knight is dead at Shrewsbury, but then he gets to his feet – a comic adventure in itself sometimes – and claims for his own the victory Hal has earned over Hotspur. For nearly three centuries, with *Part One* usually being played by itself, the plot ended with Hotspur defeated and Falstaff claiming victory. It is no wonder that the play was regarded both as historical romance with Hotspur as its centre of heroic pathos and as a comedy with Falstaff as its presiding spirit.

Part Two was occasionally performed in the same repertory as *Part One* during the seventeenth and eighteenth centuries, but the change of emphasis that makes Prince Hal the central character requires *Henry V* as well, and there is no evidence that the three plays were performed as a sequence during the first 250 years of their existence. The first recorded cycle of Shakespearian histories was produced by the nineteenth-century German director Franz Dingelstedt, who began with *1 Henry IV* in Munich in 1851 and gradually built up a connected series of seven histories over the next thirteen years (Williams, *Shakespeare on the German Stage*, pp. 153-4; Sarlos, pp. 117-31). Dingelstedt had moved to Weimar by the time his series was complete, and there the 1864 tercentenary celebration of Shakespeare's birth was centred on something the English theatre would not attempt for another 100 years (and then most of the English would think they were first), a series of *seven* successive Shakespearian histories played in rotation, the entire cycle taking a week to perform.

The English began with smaller cycles. If we define 'cycle' as three or more connected plays, the first recorded one in England was staged by Frank Benson at Stratford-upon-Avon in 1905-06. But Benson cut and rearranged the plays severely and even left *1 Henry IV* out of the fullest version of the series, preferring *Part Two* as a link between *Richard II* and *Henry V*. The Benson cycles – there were several combinations, sometimes including Marlowe's *Edward II* – certainly drew attention, and W. B. Yeats left behind an admiring comment that is still cherished at the Shakespeare Centre in Stratford about how one play supports another. But Benson's idea did not spread into the English theatre at large, and it cannot be deemed influential. The next notable history series occurred thirty years later in Pasadena, California, where the Community Playhouse staged successive productions of all *ten* English history plays in 1935, with one play closing before the next opened. That heroic effort probably deserves a book to itself, but if we are searching for the first virtually uncut cycle on the model of re-peatable sequences, as Wagner's *Ring* cycle is staged by the boldest opera companies, the first example we find in England is Strat-ford's contribution to the Festival of Britain in 1951, where *Richard II*, the two parts of *Henry IV*, and *Henry V* were staged on a single set by a single company in repertory fashion. That is the produc-tion that brought about the modern change in our understanding of the plays and made Prince Hal/Henry V the central character. Since then, the most influential productions of *1 Henry IV* have belonged to sequences in which the Prince, an apparent rapscal-lion, attains a well-planned maturity at the Battle of Shrewsbury, passes beyond his victory over Hotspur to the reconciliation with his father and the rejection of Falstaff in *Part Two*, then establishes further proof of royal authority in the unexpected victory over

France at Agincourt in *Henry V*.

One result of the modern emphasis on cycles is that the importance of Prince Hal/Henry V in Shakespeare's writing has become
apparent. I am not sure it has been noted before that Shakespeare
wrote more lines for this character than for any other – more than
for Hamlet, more than for Richard III, more than for Falstaff (who
comes second). But those lines for Hal/Henry V are stretched over
three plays which were not seen together in the days of 'Falstaff' or
'Hotspur' attractions, and it required the staying-power and financing of twentieth-century institutional theatre to take on the task of
staging history plays in cycles that would make Shakespeare's most
extensive study of political characterisation fully evident.

The question necessarily arises: did Shakespeare plan things
this way? Did he set out to write a cycle of plays on English history?
Did he discover the opportunity for such a cycle somewhere in the
course of writing the individual plays? Or – a heretical thought
today – did he remain unconcerned about a cycle all along, leaving
the whole idea to be discovered 300 to 400 years later under the
pressures of Germanic bardolatry, scholarly study, and Festivals of
Britain? Not for an instant should it be thought that these questions can be answered. The producers of the modern cycles have
claimed they were following Shakespeare's intentions, but the earlier producers of the individual 'Falstaff' and 'Hotspur' plays were
sure of his intentions too, and so were most scholars through the
ages – Shakespeare's 'intentions' being a hyperuranian lucky-bag
that one can dip into for a boost of confidence on any occasion. As
with most matters before he drew up his will (and even that raises
problems), Shakespeare left no record of his intentions – certainly
none about the 'cycle'.

In the absence of the facts, scholars have been able to speak
freely about the implications of the plays themselves. Some have
found a grand design connecting not only *Part One* to *Part Two* but
also this two-part play to *Richard II* before it and *Henry V* after it.
This is the series staged at Stratford in 1951 and it has become
known as the 'second tetralogy' among cycle advocates, the other
'tetralogy' being the three parts of *Henry VI* and *Richard III*, which
Shakespeare wrote earlier. In 1964, when the Royal Shakespeare
Company celebrated the 400th anniversary of Shakespeare's birth,
they caught up with the Weimar example of 100 years earlier by
staging both tetralogies, the eight plays being boiled down to seven
thanks to some shrewd cutting and rewriting in the earlier pieces.

[4]

Behind these cycles of 1951 and 1964 lay a work of scholarship that was influential in forming the 'grand design' theory, E. M. W. Tillyard's *Shakespeare's History Plays*. Behind *that* lay something more profound, the real source of the scholarly and theatrical 'grand design' thinking in England. I refer to the English experience of the Second World War and the desire to assert the continuing dominance of the nation's culture after the devastation of the German bombings.

This combination of nationalism, scholarship, and theatre production has left a deep impression. It is virtually impossible for a major London company to stage *1 Henry IV* today without at least wishing to connect that play to something besides itself and make a cycle of some sort. Moreover, the ambition to perform history cycles has spread to North America. It is a sign of the change I am discussing that Stratford, Ontario performed a major cycle of the histories between 1964 and 1967 in celebration of the Canadian centenary; that Ashland, Oregon connected *Richard II* and the two parts of *Henry IV* over three seasons between 1970 and 1972; that the CSC Repertory Company in New York did the same three plays in one season in 1979; and that the US Naval Academy reduced those three plus *Henry V* into two plays in 1984. Cycle-thinking has been on the upswing. Although recent scholarly opinion has rejected Tillyard's broader claims about the design of the two tetralogies, the general opinion remains tilted towards a belief that if the author's intentions could be known, they would show Shakespeare to have been something of a cycle-thinker too, albeit one who discovered some of the connections as he went along.

Shakespeare's own acting company probably did not stage anything like a cycle. Even two-part plays, of which there were many in the Elizabethan period, were not always performed on successive days. Such evidence as remains about the day-by-day Elizabethan repertory – none of it from Shakespeare's company, incidentally – shows that two-part plays such as Marlowe's *Tamburlaine* were staged in tandem less often than as separate pieces. Nothing from the Elizabethan theatre suggests that the better part of a week of a busy commercial repertory would have been given over to a series of plays in one vein. Variety was the hallmark of the repertory system. Whatever we claim about the intentions of the author, it is unlikely that Shakespeare's company ever gave him a first or second tetralogy in successive performances. What has happened to the *Henrys* in the institutional theatre since 1951 is probably a true

English innovation (the producers do not seem to have known of the German examples), and our nervous claims about following Shakespeare's intentions might as well give way to an admission that the modern Shakespearian theatre has been branching out on its own.

* * *

In the theatre of the Restoration and eighteenth century, it was hard not to approve of Falstaff. The moral earnestness by which the modern age has come to regard him as dangerous and wicked may be a return to Elizabethan thinking, as some scholars maintain, but the ages in between found him funny and sometimes grand. Joseph Addison approved of him in 1711 because 'he turns the ridicule on him that attacks him', Corbyn Morris in 1744 because 'he is happy himself and makes you happy', Samuel Johnson in 1765 because 'his licentiousness is not so offensive but that it may be borne for his mirth', although there is an additional Johnsonian note that 'neither wit nor honesty ought to think themselves safe with such a companion' (Hemingway, pp. 404-5). In the later eighteenth century Maurice Morgann wrote the first extended study of a Shakespearian character, the first in the mode of psychological essays that treat characters as though they are real persons. He did not inquire whether Hamlet was able to make up his mind or Lady Macbeth was obsessed with infantile guilt. He inquired if Falstaff was truly a coward – and found that he was vigorous, amiable, and courageous. Actors knew well enough not to bother with this deeper consideration, and they went on portraying Falstaff as a coward, albeit one confident enough to turn cowardice to his advantage. At the end of *Part One*, when he converts his battlefield fears into a stolen reputation for bravery and becomes the hero of the Battle of Shrewsbury, it is hard not to agree that such panache deserves admiration. Even Prince Hal seems a bit appreciative. So long as *1 Henry IV* was staged by itself, there was certainly little reason to think that someone so adept and amusing should be *rejected*.

The history cycles staged since the Second World War, however, have been rife with rejection for Falstaff. Turning the old man aside is a key manoeuvre in Hal's growth to political power. The actual rejection occurs in *Part Two*, but the *Part One* play-acting scene at the Boar's Head, where Falstaff and Hal take turns acting the role of King, is one of the fixing-points for productions today, because the eventual rejection is being prefigured as Hal takes the mock crown from Falstaff and mounts the mock throne. In the 1951 cycle, Richard Burton's Hal grew vehement and intense as he hurled the series of epithets against Falstaff, 'that trunk of humours, that bolting-hutch of beastliness, that swollen parcel of dropsies', and so on, to 'wherein villainous, but in all things? Wherein worthy, but in nothing' (II. iv. 431-42). The rejection was virtually occurring already in Burton's growing seriousness of tone, and it is now standard in the theatre to use the final lines of the exchange – Hal's 'I do, I will' in answer to Falstaff's 'Banish plump Jack and banish all the world' – as a profound moment of realisation, on everyone's part, that Falstaff will suffer rejection when the moment is ripe for Hal's royal personality to be declared.

The theatre of the eighteenth and early nineteenth centuries greeted this profound episode by cutting it entirely. The tavern scene 'is vastly too long', declared the acting version published in 1773, which goes back to James Quin's version of the earlier eighteenth century on this point: 'therefore it is curtailed of a mock trial the author introduced; which rather checked and loaded the main business, notwithstanding a vein of pure comedy runs through it' (Odell, II, 41). In other words, it is funny but not funny enough, and what stands in the way of the comedy is the play-acting, which we find the centre of importance. The King's role also suffered major cuts in the early eighteenth century. Betterton's version of 1700, for example, reduced the opening speech to ten lines, and forty-five of the King's lines were cut from his later interview with Prince Hal (III. ii – Hemingway, p. 502). These political elements were gradually restored during the first half of the nineteenth century, although it is reported that Abraham Lincoln, for one, still wondered why the play-acting scene should be cut (Sprague, *Shakespeare's Histories*, pp. 62-3).

The other major episode to be reduced during much of the eighteenth and nineteenth centuries was the Welsh scene, III. i, in which the rebel leaders argue over the division of the kingdom and things are brought to a calmer close by the singing of Lady Mortimer. The Betterton version of 1700 kept the quarrel between the men but ended the scene before the entrance of the women, thus avoiding the need to write the Welsh dialogue and song for Lady Mortimer, but also avoiding one of the few decent moments for actresses in the entire play. The 1773 edition cut the entire Glendower episode, calling it 'a wild scene ... which is properly rejected in the representation' (Odell, II, 41). To a modern way of thinking, again, such an opinion is hard to credit. The Welsh scene fleshes out the rebellion by showing how its leaders act when they are apart from the King and free to be themselves, but its true brilliance is the elaborate confidence of the writing, especially when the women come in. To introduce Lady Mortimer and the issue of her Welsh language may be unnecessary to the narrative, but it deepens the characterisation and ideas of the rebel side. Then to pursue that elaboration to the interlude of the song – where Welsh takes over the theatre in music and word, putting rebellion to rest for a minute – is to let an inner voice sound against the main business of political scheming. It is a difficult scene to stage, with its music, its call for a distinct female role which does not appear elsewhere, the ability in Welsh that is required. Life in the theatre is easier without these inner voices, but not as good. What I have called the confidence of the writing is actually confidence in a theatre company. I take this scene as a sign that Shakespeare's company was very certain of itself and its audience by the later 1590s, and the elimination of the Welsh scene during the thriving theatre of the eighteenth century may indicate how unusual it is to reach that stage of company development.

The earlier nineteenth century gradually restored the text of these scenes and added a new element to the play. Falstaff and Hotspur were still the main roles, but now they were joined by the astonishing technology that developed in the theatre and was capable of drawing audiences for its own sake. A production at Covent Garden in 1824 was advertised by a listing of the scenery one would surely go out of one's way to see (Odell, II, 174). 'Shrewsbury from the Field of Battle' was one of these – a distant view of Shrewsbury itself in perspective behind the battle that bears its name. (The Old Vic production of 1945, the first to be described in this book, was still using such a view, although in other respects it had been freed of elaborate scenery.) The victory over Hotspur would be concluded by an impression of sunset in the Victorian theatre, although this was not as stunning as the other major lighting opportunity, moonlight for the Gadshill robbery. Stages were enlarged to serve as arenas for these visual effects, and for episodes like the Battle of Shrewsbury enormous crowd scenes became the fashion. For the 1864 London tercentenary celebration, with *Part One* being done by itself, the Drury Lane stage filled with what looked like real armies by the fifth act: 'The Shrewsbury battle-field was divided by a long ridge, and the numerous combatants, arrayed in bright armour, were concealed under its shelter, until, rising from the ambush, they filled the stage with their glittering figures, all in vivid action and stirring conflict' (*Illustrated London News*, 2 April 1864). By this time, the Welsh scene and the play-acting segment had been restored, so it was virtually the full text that was being treated to such sumptuousness.

The twentieth-century theatre brought a reaction against Victorian pictorialism. Scenic realism and large-scale archaeological reconstructions were found to be cloying, and research into the original conditions of Elizabethan theatres showed that Shakespeare wrote for a relatively unadorned stage on which scenes could follow one another at rapid pace. Scenic effects were recognised to be in the language of the plays. The technology of the previous age was retained, of course, but it now served the interests of streamlined and supple designs which allowed directors and designers to create non-realistic environments for their productions. Quickening the pace of Shakespearian staging also opened the way for the combined performances of the two parts of *Henry IV* on the same day – not quite up to a cycle but pointing the way. Barry Jackson staged the two parts of *Henry IV* on the same day at the Birmingham Repertory Theatre in 1921, and the Stratford Memorial company performed the two parts in matinée–evening combination in 1932 to celebrate the opening of their new theatre. These double-bills were special events, but they indicate an increasing tendency in modern repertory companies to include *Part Two* in the same repertory as *Part One*.

The first production I have chosen to describe, John Burrell's for the Old Vic in 1945, reflects these twentieth-century developments: a simplified stage design (apart from Shrewsbury) and the inclusion of *Part Two* in repertory with *Part One*. Ralph Richardson's performance as Falstaff became legendary, especially because of the dimension *Part Two* gave him: he could combine the traditional comedy of *Part One* with forebodings of the rejection to follow in the next play. While this was a modern production in design and directorial conception, however, it also belonged to the centuries-old tradition of centring on famous actors in the roles of Hotspur and Falstaff. Laurence Olivier as Hotspur and Richardson as Falstaff drew most of the attention, although they were in fact surrounded by a first-rate Old Vic ensemble. Prince Hal did not attract much comment.

The giant step to a cycle was taken by the Shakespeare Memorial Theatre Company in 1951, which staged the second tetralogy, running from *Richard II* through *Henry V*, under the direction of Anthony Quayle. This is the production which established the cycle format as the modern mode for the histories. I devote a chapter to it, then follow with a chapter on the 1964 Stratford cycle of seven histories, which raised Peter Hall's new Royal Shakespeare Company to world-wide influence. I then turn to Terry Hands' 1975 four-play cycle (three *Henrys* plus *The Merry Wives of Windsor*) for a scaled-down Royal Shakespeare Company, which emphasised the psychological anxieties that might be thought to obtain between a royal father and a royal son. That series hardly brought the Royal Shakespeare Company's engagement with history cycles to a close, but some signs of strain apparent in the institutional surroundings of the 1975 production suggest that the excitement and fresh thinking of 1951 and 1964 could not be expected to last forever in one organisation.

My final chapters, accordingly, describe productions of different kinds: film and television versions, and a cycle without a home of its own. The film is Orson Welles' *Chimes at Midnight* of 1966, which usefully contradicts the expansionist tendency of the cycles by condensing the Falstaff plays into one two-hour viewing. This may look like a return to the Falstaff-centred productions of the past, but by my interpretation Welles is actually displacing Falstaff through cinematic technique, and by anyone's interpretation the film matters more for its wordless episodes than for its portrayal of any one character. Its achievement concerns the film medium *per se*, and I have included in this chapter a comparison of Welles' achievement to the BBC television version of 1979, which seems to me a failure because it refuses to do what Welles did so well, use the potential of the medium. The best feature of the BBC version is its preservation of Anthony Quayle's Falstaff, for Quayle had also played the role in the 1951 cycle, and by the time the BBC version was made, his was one of the most settled and assured Falstaffs of which we have any record at all.

Chapter VII returns to cycles by way of the irreverent version given by a new company in the mid-1980s, the English Shakespeare Company. Beginning from conditions that could hardly promise success – no theatre of their own, for example – this troupe opened with a *1 Henry IV* that brushed the usual pieties about Shakespeare and history into the dustbin. This was part of a cycle

[10]

of *1 and 2 Henry IV* plus *Henry V* from the start, but within a year of their initial success, the company expanded the cycle to seven plays, each of them disturbing the usual notions of how these pieces should be staged. Thus they were covering the same immense territory that the Royal Shakespeare Company covered in 1964 – eight of Shakespeare's histories performed as seven plays – but they were doing the entire cycle on the road, venturing across large portions of the world, and shattering some of the settled images of English history. I fancy that in touring foreign countries with their own account of English history they were imitating Henry V more closely than the anti-royalist outlook of their productions should have allowed them to do, but they also retained an admirable sense of Eastcheap attitudes: they were still without a theatre of their own, for example, and were still ready to overturn settled opinions. That is to say, *they* hadn't rejected Falstaff and his point of view even while they employed something of Henry V's overseas ambitions.

* * *

A word should be added here about the theatre as an institution, for the book that follows pays some attention to this topic. The Old Vic production of 1945 was connected to efforts behind the scenes to turn the Richardson–Olivier–Burrell company into the nucleus of the long-sought National Theatre. The Stratford cycle of 1951 was part of the transformation that was brought about at the Shakespeare Memorial Theatre after the war. The 1963-64 cycle brought a new Royal Shakespeare Company out of the Stratford organisation and helped it become the most influential English company of the 1960s. The 1975 cycle served to resolve a financial crisis in the same company. I have not hesitated to refer to the institutional politics discernible behind productions of our play, although my primary concern is to describe what happened on stage and how that was received in the audience. The play's the thing, to be sure, although Hamlet's famous line goes straight on to a remark about the conscience of the King; and that alignment of the theatrical and the political is worth retaining.

The politics of the institutional theatre are not exactly remote from the politics in *1 Henry IV*. The modern subsidised theatre helps cycles be staged, and cycles make Falstaff a figure to be rejected. That is what happens to *1 Henry IV* in its modern cycle-oriented treatments: the Prince grows into royal authority by turning aside the old fat man, and it is government subsidy that provides the wherewithal – some of the wherewithal, because it is never enough – to let this lesson be dramatised.

Theatre people will know that this cannot be the final word. The theatre is too subversive for that. For one thing, the shift to cycle-thinking that has occurred in the institutional theatre has not caused isolated productions of *1 Henry IV* to dwindle among smaller companies. *1 Henry IV* continues to be performed as a single play throughout the English-speaking world, and I would imagine that most readers of this book first encountered it that way – without the actual rejection of Falstaff, and without the Prince becoming a King. I saw my first production – and worked on it, too – in an American university in the 1950s. We took on *1 Henry IV* because it was a great challenge. The play requires a larger capable company than do most of the comedies and tragedies, but it also requires what the comedies and tragedies always require, some-thing special at the top, in this case a Falstaff who can live up to the reputation of the role, the reputation that was built up by Betterton, Quin, and the other famous Falstaffs over the long course of the English stage. We tried to stress the political roles of Prince Hal and Henry IV, for we knew what Stratford had done in 1951. Our director had read Tillyard and in part believed it. More to the point, he *played* Henry IV, and was not interested in marginalising himself. Our Falstaff was well-read too. He tried to subordinate his performance to the political design. After all, this was a university.

But Falstaff still stole the show – and he stole it because of the way the play comes to an end, with Falstaff's comic survival at the Battle of Shrewsbury and his outrageous trick of stealing Prince Hal's victory over Hotspur. That is not quite the ending, of course, but the final lines about further rebellion and so on did not make us think we ought to be staging *Part Two* as well and even looking ahead to *Henry V*. That is for the institutional theatre. Our pro-duction was complete with the closure Falstaff gave it, and I think this must still be the experience of many theatregoers. I have checked the American Shakespeare productions listed in *Shake-speare Quarterly* over recent years, and I find that *1 Henry IV* has been staged by itself in New Hampshire, Maine, Vermont, Massa-chusetts, California, Colorado, Washington, North Carolina, Illi-nois, Texas, Ohio, New Jersey, Alabama, Utah, Oregon, New York, Connecticut, Indiana, Pennsylvania, and the District of Columbia.

The list is bound to be incomplete. Every one of the United States has surely had this play on the boards in the past quarter-century, and this is not exactly North American subject matter. I would not begin to count the productions staged in the provincial repertory companies, university drama departments, and local theatres of the nation whose history Shakespeare was actually writing about, let alone the rest of the English-speaking world.

While this book is mainly about the change that has occurred in the institutional theatre, then, I have retained something of my own first experience, and perhaps that of the reader too, that Falstaff cannot be rejected so emphatically as cycle-thinkers, including Shakespeare if he was one, would ask us to believe he should. The productions described in the last two chapters of this book are vastly different in most respects, but two of them are alike in preserving a sort of Falstaffian artistry. Orson Welles was practising some Falstaffian ruses as producer of *Chimes at Midnight*, as Chapter VI will indicate, and I believe the extraordinary visual rhythm of the film comes from an artistic imagination that resembles Falstaff's way of seeing the world. His rejection by Prince Hal is dutifully shown (again and again, as it turns out), but the Falstaffian way of seeing, if I am right about it, is inherent in the technique of the film and cannot be eliminated. As for the English Shakespeare Company, another aspect of Falstaff lies behind the iconoclasm of their version of English history, but I also have in mind the interaction between the director, Michael Bogdanov, and John Woodvine, who played Falstaff. I believe my impression is shared by others that these two were not a perfect match, the one an actor experienced in the classics, the other a director antagonistic to classicism; and the wonderful Falstaff that resulted had an air of negotiation about him, as though good theatre could be produced by people who learn from one another without losing their individuality. This Falstaff was rejected in the cycle too, of course, but it was too late. He had already arrived to stay in the planning stages, as an attitude of risk-taking and anti-establishment thinking that directors and actors can build on. It is a pleasure to let this survey of *1 Henry IV* come to a close with a company that carried a scandalous version of English history the world over – cultural imperialists to be sure, but impious ones, prepared to act as though Jack Falstaff and the theatre could still co-operate in the spirit of Misrule.

CHAPTER II

1945. The Old Vic:
Olivier–Richardson–Burrell

The standard-bearer of British theatre in the immediate aftermath of the Second World War was the Old Vic Company, as it was reorganised in 1944 with Ralph Richardson, Laurence Olivier, and John Burrell as artistic directors. The Old Vic already had a firm reputation for Shakespeare and other classical drama, but the company formed in 1944 had a special purpose. It would demonstrate that the London theatre had not only survived the years of devastating air-raids but had survived with unmatchable ability. The Old Vic Theatre itself had been bombed early in the war and was still unusable for productions, but the company had taken a lease at a West End playhouse, the New, and their plan was to perform a repertory of classical plays on the continental model, with productions rehearsed simultaneously and performed in rotation. The continental system had never been successful in the modern London theatre, but now it would take hold. The company would be highlighted by Olivier and Richardson, who were both thought to be reaching the peaks of their careers (those careers had several peaks, as it turned out), yet it would also demonstrate the depth and versatility required through the ranks for this kind of repertory. The war was not over – indeed, a resurgence of air attacks occurred in 1944 – but even in a darkened London the Old Vic would prove that the English theatre was continuous and strong.

Shakespeare was essential to this demonstration of cultural superiority. The British survived the German bombings and threats of invasion with many forms of resilience, courage, and stubbornness: keeping Shakespeare on the boards was one of these. Donald Wolfit gave lunchtime scenes and readings in the Strand Theatre, which had had its back wall and dressing–rooms blown out by bombs. Full-length performances were often interrupted from the air, and at one performance of *Hamlet*, the audience was startled to hear anti-aircraft guns begin to fire just when Fortinbras said, 'Go, bid the soldiers shoot' (Trewin, pp. 182-97). The Old Vic company itself had been forced to evacuate to Burnley after their theatre was bombed, but with the support of the newly formed Committee for the Encouragement of Music and the Arts (the forerunner of the present Arts Council) they turned necessity to advantage by branching out on several regional tours which carried Shakespeare far from London and gave the impression of a unified national culture. One troupe, headed by Sybil Thorndike and Lewis Casson, played *Macbeth* in thirty-eight Welsh towns in ten weeks, with Dame Sybil doubling Lady Macbeth and the First Witch for audiences largely composed of miners. Shakespeare was helping to preserve the nation. 'The theatre in particular is a necessity to a nation which wishes to consider itself civilized', wrote Tyrone Guthrie of the early wartime years (quoted in Harcourt Williams, p. 167), and towards the end, Edward J. Dent summed up the sense of cultural survival by saying that the Bible may have faded as the one book which every Englishman knew, but Shakespeare 'stands safe and unshaken' (Dent, p. 11).

So the reshaped Old Vic company of 1944 would be expected to make something special of Shakespeare. It was a sign of the company's depth and confidence, as well as of the politics of the moment, that their first three Shakespeare productions were English histories: *Richard III* in the 1944-45 season, and the two parts of *Henry IV* in 1945-46. Staging Shakespeare's versions of fifteenth-century English history was a statement in itself about the continuation of English history in 1944 and 1945. Moreover, the histories, crowded with speaking parts and unsparing to the performer of the small role, are the most challenging kind of Shakespeare for proving the assurance of an overall company. Sir Walter Blunt has only a handful of speeches in *1 Henry IV*, for example, but each of them is risky and distinct (his first speech tries to correct the King in a moment of royal wrath – I. iii. 70-6 – and his third, some two hours later, delivers the King's offer of negotiation to the rebels in a complex mixture of serviceableness and disdain –

[15]

IV. iii. 30-51). One of the lesser actors of a company will be assigned this part, and he will have little room for building credibility. He must be instantly the seasoned and adroit political functionary, one whom the Court trusts and uses, to Blunt's very great cost eventually. If the actor should falter, the rest of the Court looks a little silly for needing him as they do. The histories are filled with roles like this, small but demanding parts on which the credibility of others depends. The Old Vic was able to assign Sir Walter Blunt to George Curzon, who had been acting steadily in London for twenty years, and whose other roles in the repertory of 1945-46 were Creon in *Oedipus Rex*, Sneer in Sheridan's *The Critic*, and Scroop in *2 Henry IV*. The company consisted of veterans like Curzon, Nicholas Hannen, George Relph, Sybil Thorndike, and Harcourt Williams, along with relative newcomers like Joyce Redman, who had been acting in London for a decade, and Margaret Leighton, just down from provincial repertory.

I mention the depth of the company because just about everyone who remembers the famous post-war Old Vic thinks of Olivier and Richardson first of all, and it is hard to get beyond these two headliners. They were famous for their stage roles, famous for their films. They were stars. Both had to be released from the Fleet Air Arm to join the 1944 company, but it was understood that performing Shakespeare and other classics was a more important contribution to the war effort than they could make in uniform. (Olivier had just finished his film of *Henry V*, with its heroic version of earlier English victories across the Channel, another part of the wartime morale-boosting effort.) So it was arranged for the two well-known actors to leave the service and join the director John Burrell at the head of the Old Vic company.

Rehearsals took place during the air raids of 1944. In an empty hall of the National Gallery, the pictures having been removed for safe keeping, the company read through *Richard III* and *Peer Gynt*, hesitating upon the sound of rockets coming over. The ones you could hear, it was said, were the ones that wouldn't kill you (Williams, 1949, p. 177). From such beginnings came a famous first season. *Richard III* and *Peer Gynt* were deep-spirited productions, still remembered and influential today for Olivier's title-performance in the first and Richardson's in the second, but with good acting throughout the large casts. The first season also included strong productions of Shaw's *Arms and the Man* and Chekhov's *Uncle Vanya*, the latter showing what good ensemble performers Olivier (Astrov) and Richardson (Vanya) also were.

The war finally ended during that first season, and by the time *1 Henry IV* opened the second one, in September 1945, the theatre seemed to be part of a new age in London culture. One must imagine the pleasure of going to the theatre without worrying about air-raids for a change – and the pleasure, too, of knowing that in the centre of an active commercial theatre, the best actors could be seen in a rotation of classical plays at prices most people could afford. In the larger world, where the Labour Party had swept to power on a promise of a new democratic social order, the end to austerity was at least imaginable. Strikes, shortages, and dire cold in the next few years brought such optimism to an end, but it was there for a while, blending disparate elements of the culture together, and the Old Vic was part of the impression that something immensely successful was going on. When *1 Henry IV* opened in September 1945, under Burrell's direction and with Richardson as Falstaff and Olivier as Hotspur, it was clear that the British theatre had not only survived the war, but had survived with what was arguably the best theatre company in the world performing what were arguably the plays of the greatest dramatist in history. Some there were who thought Shakespeare had helped to defeat Germany.

* * *

What did not occur at the Old Vic was much fresh thinking. The cultural conditions outlined above tended to sharpen the conservative instincts of cultural strongholds like the Old Vic, and the innovations of their productions were largely a matter of individual touches applied by Olivier and Richardson. In some respects the reorganised Old Vic was a return to the actor–manager tradition of earlier ages in the English theatre, where the most famous performers administered their own companies, supervised the productions, and took the leading parts. Olivier and Richardson were thought capable of all these activities. John Burrell, the youngest member of the triumvirate and certainly the least famous, actually did the work of administration. He was also the best director of the triumvirate, but it was not for him to impose an overall directorial conception on productions featuring Olivier and Richardson, at least not so that anyone would notice. The time yet lay ahead when English directors would publish their interpretations in the press and become the spokesmen for their own work.

Thus Burrell's production of *1 Henry IV* was swift and secure, without a trace of unconventionality. This was straightforward proscenium staging in the modern streamlined tradition, where location was established not so often by a change of set as by a change of backcloth and drape. The only big pictorial vista in the Old Vic production was the Battle of Shrewsbury, which employed a pastoral scene of fields leading to a distant church-spire, the sort of visual literalism that now appears sentimental. No one said it was out of place as a background for the heroic death-throes Olivier gave to Hotspur, to be described shortly.

The fanfare-like music, composed by Herbert Menges and played live, drew admiring comment. The rhythm of the production was to segment each scene clearly with music and a change of background, and to keep up a rapid pace of dialogue within each segment. Several London reviewers thought the dialogue too quick, but they were clearly favouring the deliberate elocution of a pre-war Shakespearianism that the Old Vic Company was prepared to render *passé*. Brisk assurance in the staging and speech is what this company sought, and by 1945 they had attained it. Running-time was under three hours. As was traditional, the Carriers' scene (II. i) and the Archbishop's colloquy with 'Sir Michael' (IV. iv) were cut. (Burrell must have intended to do the Carriers' scene, for blocking and internal cuts are marked in the prompt-book, now at the University of Bristol, but then the entire scene was crossed out.) The first interval fell after sixty-nine minutes, at the end of the first tavern scene. Then followed two shorter parts, each running to about forty minutes, divided after III.iii, the second tavern scene.

The keynotes of a production of *1 Henry IV* are often sounded by the King himself, who is never seen to be free from one of his two crises – the political crisis of rebellion by the northern lords, and the personal crisis of rebellion by his apparently wayward son. A father or a king might be expected to crack a little under such stress, especially a king who has usurped the crown. We will see that later productions drew upon the opportunities for disturbance in the role, making Henry himself part of the problem of the realm. In the Old Vic production, however, Nicholas Hannen's King was the sort of conscientious, well-meaning parent and ruler we would all desire to be under the circumstances: 'anxious indeed to preserve peace in his kingdom, but also a father saddened by the dissolute fecklessness of his heir and eldest son, trying with patience and an almost wistful disappointment to bridge the rift'

[18]

(Williamson, pp. 183-4).

Such normality at the centre of authority is bound to have an effect on other major roles. The rebellion of the northern lords gains a useful measure of theatrical justification when the King is abrasive and unfair, but Hannen's subdued, decent Henry rendered him unavailable to the rebels as a personal foil. The political reasons for the rebellion were preserved without serious cuts, but *1 Henry IV* offers no convenient summary of the political issues, which are introduced gradually through the personal interactions of the characters. If the King will not fuel a rebellion by behaving badly, one can always turn to that unfailing source of disorderly ambition according to some romantic temperaments, oneself. Hotspur is a role ripe for such inspiration, and we shall see that Olivier was quick to realise the opportunity to portray a self-sufficient rebel. The other inspired rebel ego in this production belonged to Owen Glendower. Harcourt Williams seized the role's tendency towards unearthly mysticism in III. i –

> at my birth
> The frame and huge foundation of the earth
> Shaked like a coward (14-16) –

and created a figure possessed. What he was possessed by was a matter of some dispute – by demons according to one observer (Williamson, p. 186) and by 'eloquent hocus-pocus' according to another (*Observer*, 30 September 1945). The dichotomy is just about perfect, with the first reviewer seeing the result from Glendower's point of view, the second from Hotspur's: the range of possibilities in III. i could not be bettered.

This Glendower of the glittering eye contributed to the overall impression that the rebels, while offering their fascinating individual turns, were self-indulgent and untrustworthy. The centre of stability was in the Court party. Anti-war feeling might be expected to enter into a production of 1945, and later productions would make it clear that the militarism of the Court party can be portrayed as brutal and destructive. But the Old Vic protected the King and the Prince from such an attitude, and in this regard the small role of Vernon was especially useful. Vernon is the follower of Hotspur who shows admiration for Prince Hal just before the battle, and Burrell emphasised the credibility of his feelings by making him the one rebel who was level-headed and decent. In V. ii, when Worcester insisted that the truth about the King's offer must be kept from Hotspur, Vernon was reluctant to participate in the deceit and showed signs of shame when the lie was told. But then his chance came. When asked about Hal's deportment, he burst out with pride in having such a Prince (Sprague, *Shakespearean Players and Performances*, p. 173):

> *Hotspur.* Tell me, tell me,
> How showed his tasking? Seemed it in contempt?
> *Vernon.* No, by my soul, I never in my life
> Did hear a challenge urged more modestly,
> Unless a brother should a brother dare
> To gentle exercise and proof of arms.
> He gave you all the duties of a man,
> Trimmed up your praises with a princely tongue ...
>
> (V.ii.49-56)

On he goes in praise of the Prince who is, after all, supposed to be the enemy. When later productions made Hal more ominous, Vernon seemed a little out of touch – an idealist hankering for a bygone age of chivalry – but in 1945 he was telling the truth about a Prince who made war seem chivalrous.

The one anti-war touch in 1945 centred on Falstaff. His soliloquy about his recruits ('If I be not ashamed of my soldiers, I am a soused gurnet. I have misused the King's press damnably' – IV. ii. 11-12) was accompanied by off-stage marching by the minor actors, who tramped in the wings and gave forth an exhausted 'Greensleeves'. A. C. Sprague, who saw the production in New York, remembered the tone of war-weariness: 'a Greensleeves worn down into a sort of rhythmical grumbling' (*Shakespearean Players and Performances*, pp. 171-2). Cynicism about honour and war could be understood as part of Falstaff's idiosyncrasy, it appears, without spreading to the presentation of royal authority, whose battlefield ventures seemed well justified and admirable – Vernon's view. This was not a *1 Henry IV* for downgrading English power.

* * *

The older tradition for playing *1 Henry IV*, as I have explained in the Introduction, was to cast the leading player of a company, the Betterton of the day, as Falstaff or as Hotspur. The Old Vic company, having two leads, went the tradition one better. Richardson played Falstaff, Olivier played Hotspur. Seventy-five per cent of nearly every review, and usually the first seventy-five per cent, was devoted to these two performances. The reviewers were aware that legends were being created in the post-war Old Vic company and they were prepared to join the effort.

Richardson made them remember all the other Falstaffs they had seen or heard of. This Falstaff accounted for the others and added his own quality, which was a quality of mind. J. C. Trewin could remember George Robey, Robert Atkins, and Roy Byford in the part: 'nobody of our day, however, has matched Ralph Richardson in total accomplishment' (*John O'London's Weekly*, 19 October 1945). James Agate, notoriously hard on Richardson in the past, thought the only way to do justice to this performance was to summon Hazlitt from a century before, who had said of a great Falstaff, 'when he puts himself whole into a jest, it is unrivalled' (*Sunday Times*, 30 September 1945): this could now be said of Richardson. And Alan Dent went back to Maurice Morgann's essay of 1777, which made Falstaff famous for psychological reasons, and said that Richardson had caught 'the same appearance of perfect good nature, pleasantry, mellowness, and hilarity of mind' (*News Chronicle*, 30 September 1945).

What, exactly, did he do? That the comments quoted above ring with praise which does not actually describe the performance can in part be explained by legend-making, but Richardson was a difficult actor to describe. His talent was not superficially obvious. He had nothing of Gielgud's vocal range and beauty, nothing of Olivier's physical magnetism. Men of his stature and shape knew well enough to stay off the stage. The great tragic roles were beyond him. The first thing in his favour was that he knew all of these limitations. He did not always stay within them, but he knew them. The next thing was that he had a mind for acting. When Olivier came to him and suggested that he take on Falstaff, his reaction was: 'I thought about it. I have a certain alacrity of thinking that might help me with the part.' He also said, later, 'not until you play Falstaff do you realize how small the mere actor is' (O'Conner, p. 123).

The latter quote risks sounding like false modesty, but Richardson was not given to such poses. He had a knack for meaning what he said for listeners who would think things through. 'Small' is the word to think about here. Richardson knew that if he could make himself 'small' in some sense, there would be a gap between himself and the large character he was playing, the fat knight. In that gap would lie the source of his performance. So Richardson, who was not small, made himself all the things small persons like to be – quick, agile, imaginative. He stayed up on the balls of his feet, ready to move, his eyes darting to take in the scene. Alacrity is the best word for it, and again it is Richardson's word: 'a certain alacrity of thinking'. The task was to translate the alacrity from the mind to the body.

The great Falstaff body was carefully made: Turkish towelling material next to the skin, around that a light mackintosh, and around that a layer of horsehair (without the mackintosh, Richardson said, the horsehair 'felt like an attack from a swarm of bees' – O'Conner, p. 124). Richardson's scrawny legs obviously did not belong to this outward body, so they were sculpted with silk quilting covered with light red stockings. Falstaffs had worn boots since the seventeenth century to hide the fact that the actor's legs of normal size did not go with his padded fat body (the boots can be seen in the first picture of Falstaff on stage, the frontispiece of *The Wits*, 1662 – see Bevington, p. 69), but boots were cumbersome for a conception that depended on quickness, so Richardson rejected boots and used quilted stockings instead. The costumer was Alix Stone. 'She created a complete anatomy for me in padding,' Richardson said. 'I had two or three stomachs, two or three chests, and two huge arms … .You could see the anatomy of the creature' (Burton, p. 69). The aim was to give the impression of bulk while retaining lightness, so the smaller actor could move the whole apparatus adroitly. It seemed as though the spirit was moving the flesh, when in fact it was Richardson moving horsehair.

Much of the animation came from the face. Richardson's face was round enough to belong to the padded body, especially with a flare of whiskers, but the eyes and the nose were those of the smaller man. His nose was already as sharp as a pin, wrote Ivor Brown, seeing vulnerability in the face from the beginning (quoted in Findlater, 1983, p. 125: the allusion is to the description of Falstaff's death in *Henry V*). Richardson could do wonders with his face. He could turn it red in an instant, as though anger or embarrassment dwelt on the surface of the great body, and his eyes could fix you from any angle and fool you. Orson Welles is said to have visited Richardson after one performance and told him: 'Thought I'd done all right as Falstaff but the thing I must say, Ralph, I never matched you at the end. I could never do that because I haven't got your blue eyes.' He then looked at Richardson's face, paused a minute, and said, 'By God, you haven't got blue eyes' (O'Conner, p. 125).

The one way to get this Falstaff wrong would be to overlook the inner spirit and concentrate on the outward body. That is what

Prince Hal does for a moment in the first tavern scene, when he castigates Falstaff as 'that bolting hutch of beastliness, that swollen parcel of dropsies, that huge bombard of sack, that stuffed cloak-beg of guts' (II. iv. 433-35). For a moment Hal is overlooking what the audience to Richardson's performance was learning to see, that here was 'a greatness of spirit that transcended the mere hulk of flesh' (Williamson, p. 158), or that this was 'the most dignified, the most thoughtful, and the most gentlemanly of Falstaffs' (*Observer*, 30 September 1945). Prince Hal, that is to say, did not see the legend before him. 'There was a charity about Sir Ralph's performance,' wrote Kenneth Tynan years later, 'a magnanimity and a grief, that made you wonder whether Auden's audacious hint may not be the simple truth, after all' (*Showpeople*, p. 26). Auden's 'audacious hint,' just to indicate how far spectators were willing to carry the legend, was that Falstaff is a comic symbol of Christ.

The legendary figure really behind this performance, however, was not Christ but Peer Gynt. Richardson had played Peer with great success in the previous Old Vic season (with Olivier as the Button Moulder), and the 'certain alacrity for thinking' by which he approached Falstaff included the awareness that the groundwork for the new characterisation had already been laid. He had caught the romantic story-teller in the young Peer, and he had caught the disillusionment and exhaustion of the old Peer. The child was vivid in the first, the old man in the second. For Falstaff, the job was to put the two together, rather as the large character was put together with the 'small' actor, so that this old man would light up as a child, especially when telling stories. 'Falstaff has never completely grown up', commented Audrey Williamson on Richardson's performance (p. 186); and when the company went to New York, George Jean Nathan saw the same thing, in terms that would describe Peer Gynt perfectly: Falstaff has an 'inner childish nature', along with 'paradoxical wit and stupidity at times operating in unison' (*New York Journal American*, 13 May 1946).

These qualities came together in the story Falstaff invents for Hal about what happened at Gadshill. This scene had recently been declared a problem by an influential scholar, Dover Wilson, who could not believe that Falstaff would get himself in such a jam. How could he be so foolish as to enlarge the story that way? No one of Falstaff's intelligence would increase his opponents from four to seven and from seven to eleven, making himself all the more a victim to Hal's trap. Wilson solved this problem by deciding that

[23]

Falstaff knew all along what Hal and Poins were doing to him at Gadshill, and now he is just helping them set up their trap by increasing the number of his opponents. When he tells them 'By the Lord, I knew ye as well as he that made ye' (II. iv. 258), he is telling the truth (Wilson, *Fortunes of Falstaff*, pp. 51 ff.).

Richardson played the scene in the old-fashioned way and showed that the old-fashioned way was best. His Falstaff enlarged the story because he was foolish enough to love telling stories, especially stories about himself, which would tend to grow larger in keeping with the girth of the storyteller. It was the young Peer Gynt's mind in the Falstaff body, and the conviction of Richardson's performance had been earned over two seasons. When Hal sprang the trap on him, and then demanded that he find a way to go on lying, Richardson refused the standard ploy by which Falstaffs of the past had set up their next line. The standard ploy, going back to Charles Matthews' performance in 1814, was for Falstaff to hide his face behind his shield, then slowly lower it on 'By the Lord, I knew ye as well as he that made ye', thus gaining a cute effect of peeping and saving the effort of showing the audience his initial reaction (Brown, p. 148; Sprague, *Shakespeare's Histories*, pp. 61-2). Richardson did not hide his face. His pause was prolonged, and one had to read his face – read the shock at discovering the collapse of a wonderful story and almost at once the discovery that a new story could be told: I knew you all along. That was the sign of Richardson's interpretation. He refused to be coy and insisted on showing himself as something other than a glutton. He was quicker than anyone else, but quite wrapped up in fictions that would eventually bring him down.

* * *

Olivier's Hotspur was the soldier and the lover, with the one sometimes arising when only the other was appropriate. His first scene with Margaret Leighton as Lady Percy was romantic, sexy, and charged with the impatience of a man who might rather be on horseback. His scenes with the other rebels, especially in the 'pluck up drowned honour by the locks' speech to Northumberland and Worcester (I. iii. 201-8), seemed more romantic than politically astute, as though this kind of imagination should be devoted to Margaret Leighton. Such unpredictability made Hotspur seem to be the source of his own rebelliousness – the King did not drive him to revolt, his youthfulness did not lure him into folly. This Hotspur was adroit at unruliness and proud to be unfathomable. This is not an unorthodox reading of the role. It is based on a romantic view that finds self-generated lawlessness attractive, and in the tradition of casting a star performer as Hotspur it is the most common interpretation: the character who stands apart from his surroundings places a leading player in good stead.

The uniqueness of Olivier's performance lay in the details he etched on this romantic version of Hotspur. The prompt-book shows some of his techniques. Throughout Olivier's role pauses are marked, to place him at the centre of a scene's rhythm. At IV. iii. 52, when Sir Walter Blunt offers pardon to the rebels, a triple pause is marked before Hotspur's reply, a long silence which lets him be drawn to the offer as an escape from the disaster he is bringing on himself and his followers. That would be one beat. Three beats of silence let him remember his own version of history, which carries a great charge of anger:

> *Blunt*. He bids you name your griefs, and with all speed
> You shall have your desires with interest
> And pardon absolute for yourself and these
> Herein misled by your suggestion.
> *Hotspur*. [*Triple pause*]
> The King is kind; and well we know the King
> Knows at what time to promise, when to pay.
> My father and my uncle and myself
> Did give him that same royalty he wears,
> And when he was not six-and-twenty strong,
> Sick in the world's regard, wretched and low,
> A poor unminded outlaw sneaking home,
> My father gave him welcome to the shore; ... (IV. iii. 48-59)

That is one way of gaining the spotlight. Another is the pin-up pose. At the beginning of II. iii, 'Enter Hotspur solus, reading a letter', Olivier elevated one booted foot on to a chair so that his doublet would be hiked up a little and his legs, in tight hose, nicely exposed. This may seem a bit statuesque for Hotspur, and other positions are possible. In *Chimes at Midnight*, for example, Orson Welles would have Hotspur read his letter while soaking in a bath, then get out and drop the letter in the water. In the recent English Shakespeare Company production, John Price, naked to the waist, would glance at the letter while shaving. But these were bawdy, down-to-earth Hotspurs. The lathered face and bare torso would not have been appropriate for Olivier, whose Hotspur was outwardly composed and elegant. A ginger beard and moustache edged the fea-

[25]

tures of this well-known face. His doublet and hose fit tightly. This was a medieval knight looking like an Elizabethan courtier awaiting the invention of photography. The challenge was to be risqué without losing elegance, and the solution was a touch of male cheesecake. So up went the boot on to the chair in the letter scene.

Hotspur as the romantic hero requires a memorable death. The stage at the New was built up with risers, and Olivier received his death blow on the second step. He remained upright through most of his final speech ('O Harry, thou hast robbed me of my youth!' – V. iv. 76), partly obscuring Hal, who remained behind him. His hand clutched at his neck as he spoke. Blood poured through his fingers. At 'No, Percy, thou art dust', he plunged down the two steps and fell, as two observers recalled, 'onto his face' (Findlater, *These Our Actors*, p. 93; Speaight, *Shakespeare on the Stage*, p. 230).

For the full effect of his death, however, one must consider the voice. Nearly every first-night reviewer wrote about the slight stammer Olivier gave to Hotspur, to which we will return, and many also noticed that he spoke so rapidly as to be sometimes incomprehensible. Throughout his career Olivier was charged with failing to speak verse well. The accusations came from those who believed in the older elocutionary style which he was deliberately casting off. It was Olivier's way of setting himself off from John Gielgud, the master of the elocutionary school. Olivier's own description would have us believe he was being 'naturalistic' in these endeavours (*On Acting*, pp. 69-75), but in his search for the voice of each character, he was being no more naturalistic than he was in his search for the face of each character, over which he also spent much preparation. He was looking for the magnet in the face or the voice, the piece of individuality that would rivet attention on the unique theatricality of the performance, and only on occasion did that unique theatricality also happen to seem 'natural'.

The Hotspur voice was warm and impulsive except for the slight stammer on the letter 'w', and it went with the hint of fire in the ginger wig, beard, and moustache, which, it is said, Olivier spent three hours putting on each night (Speaight, *Shakespeare on the Stage*, p. 230). His critics couldn't understand some of the lines, but his admirers knew that a great Shakespearian voice was being made in this actor's career, and in this Hotspur they were even able to hear music and precious metal. As Audrey Williamson put it, Hotspur 'revealed less a voice than a full instrumentation of vibrancy and colour. The rhetoric poured forth like molten silver' (p.

184).

As for the stammer, everyone noticed it and most reviewers thought Olivier invented it: 'an almost imperceptible hesitation before the letter w' (*The New Yorker*, 18 May 1946); 'a perpetually amusing seizure of the upper lip' (*The Tatler and Bystander*, 10 October 1945). But Hotspurs had stammered throughout the twentieth century. Matheson Lang had stammered in the Beerbohm Tree production of 1914, Baliol Holloway stammered in 1923, Gyles Isham in 1931, all because of a misunderstanding of Lady Percy's comment in *Part Two* that her husband had a 'blemish' of speaking 'thick' (Sprague, *Shakespeare's Histories*, p. 57). This actually means that he spoke rapidly, as in 'thick and fast,' but it was taken to mean a stammer in 1914, and a stammer it remained for generations. By speaking rapidly most of the time and by stammering now and then, Olivier was having it both ways.

None of the earlier Hotspurs had had the brilliance to realise where the stammer, if there was to be one, should fall. Olivier was the first to introduce it on 'w' – a slight hesitation, but enough for everyone to notice. Prince Hal noticed, and his parody of Hotspur at II. iv. 102 included a jibe at the blemish: 'Fie upon this quiet life! I w-w-want w-w-work.' But the reason for 'w' came at the end. Shakespeare has Hotspur die before he can say his last word, which would have been 'worms' in the phrase 'food for worms,' but Olivier's Hotspur tried to say it and died on the stammer. Hal, waiting, finished the line gently for him:

> *Hotspur.* No, Percy, thou art dust,
> And food for w-w-
> *Prince.* For worms, brave Percy. (V. iv. 84-6)

It was a fine touch of the theatre, an actor revealing what is not exactly there. Even James Agate, who was sometimes hard on Olivier's performances, found this ending graced 'with a noble pathos' (*Sunday Times*, 30 September 1945). Olivier often tried larger and grander ways of drawing out what he found latent in Shakespeare, but he never found anything so precise as this small trick of the lip.

* * *

I have mentioned that Nicholas Hannen's portrayal of the King as a decent, straightforward ruler made the rebellion against him less justifiable. The rebel who matters most in this regard, however, is the apparent rebel in the royal family, Prince Hal. The possibilities for playing a troubled Hal seem rich today, thanks to the variations of gloomy self-regard, icy malice, and neurotic self-pity that have been performed by later actors, but the later actors were able to play against fathers who imposed themselves on their sons in some dominating way, making Hal's inner rebellion seem a reaction to real paternal pressure. Michael Warre's Hal in 1945 did not have such psychological depth, and although this was partly because the role was being played down to keep the focus on the lead performances of Richardson and Olivier, it was also because a Hal whose father is well-meaning, kind, sincere, and decent – sad about his son, of course, but patient through it all – really is not a rebellious Hal, for he has nothing to rebel against. He is just doing what he says he is doing: being crafty, pretending to deviate from courtly behaviour in order to make the nation hearken to his 'reformation' when the time is right.

That is exactly what Hal says his motives are in the 'I know you all' soliloquy at the end of his first scene (I. ii); the later anxiety-ridden Hals, it is worth noting, have had to develop a sub-text for this speech in order to trouble its surface of political calculation with deeper, unacknowledged feelings related to the father. Warre was in the interesting position of taking the soliloquy at its word, playing a Hal whose rebellion is only a façade. What the actor of such a Hal has to work with in the 'I know you all' soliloquy is a carefully planned rhetorical shift. Hal has been speaking in prose throughout the scene (I. ii), as he banters with Falstaff and Poins and agrees to join the Gadshill exploit. The soliloquy shifts the mode to blank verse, and an experienced actor can make that change in itself a point of interest, revealing now a second method of speech in Hal, a much more formal method, and one that he seems to reserve for talking to himself. That he is confiding in a theatre audience when he talks to himself also adds a dimension to the role, for a soliloquy (whether or not it is directly spoken to the spectators) always treats the audience to confidentiality. The Hal of 'I know you all' is thus in touch with the crowd of the audience even as he seems to be distancing himself from that Eastcheap crowd of Falstaff and his cronies; and this complicated moment, which manages to include the theatrical situation as well as the fictional situation, could be as interesting as the later moody sub-textual Hals with Oedipal problems.

Of Michael Warre's Hal, however, it must be reported that no reviewer found it interesting. The rhetorical possibilities described above depend on giving Hal some of the highlighting techniques that seem to have been reserved for Hotspur and Falstaff in 1945. A soliloquy's effect of confidentiality comes across less easily in a proscenium theatre like the New than it would have on the projecting stage that Shakespeare wrote for. And although the Old Vic was a strong company down through the ranks, they did choose a relatively inexperienced actor for Hal. 'This stripling would have got the better of Hotspur only on the theory that ash can tilt successfully at oak', wrote one reviewer of Warre's Prince Hal (*Sunday Times*, 30 September 1945). That is a sign of what the actor confronted, with no paternal menace to struggle against and with Richardson and Olivier to outshine him. (Warre's real talent, it should be added, lay in stage design, where he had a fine career.) A strange twist was thus given to the basic plot. Those whom Prince Hal defeated or rejected in the two-part play (the Old Vic soon added *Part Two*) were possessed of the power of their star performers, and Hal was of interest not because he triumphed at Shrewsbury but because his actor at least survived the competition on the stage of the New. To say of Hal that he was 'highly tried' by his encounter with Hotspur and Falstaff, and that he 'comes creditably through his ordeal' (*The Tatler and Bystander*, 10 October 1945), does not cast much light on the future Henry V, but this is the best the reviewers could say of Michael Warre's encounter with Richardson and Olivier. And not everyone thought he came through. 'Promoted to play in such society as this,' sniffed the *Observer* (30 September 1945), Warre 'inevitably remains in the junior school.' Yes, the Old Vic had a strong ensemble, and the lesser roles were played with assurance, but the one character who can match the importance of Hotspur or Falstaff – the one who does, after all, succeed at their expense, killing Hotspur to conclude *Part One* and rejecting Falstaff to conclude *Part Two* – was undercast and made into the weakest feature of the production.

The play-acting between Falstaff and Hal in the first tavern scene shows the slant of the interpretation towards the star performance and away from Warre. The seriousness that has now become traditional on Hal's 'I do, I will' (II. iv. 463) as he responds to Falstaff's 'banish fat Jack and banish all the world', was not evident here. Instead, the focus remained on Falstaff. The promptbook records several touches which kept him at the centre of attention. The later Stratford interpretation isolates Falstaff from the tavern crowd as the scene builds and they sense his vulnerability to Hal's deliberateness, but Richardson held his cronies with him as his rhetoric increased, and he took Mistress Quickly by the hand on 'but for sweet Jack Falstaff, kind Jack Falstaff ...' (II. iv. 457-8). The 'I do, I will' itself was accompanied by a bit of badinage: Hal 'throws cushion on Falstaff'. It was all a game – the cushion was being used for the crown, and Hal was joshing with it. There was no sign that he sees the future in this moment, no sign, indeed, that Hal was anything but a useful assistant in a big scene for Richardson. Eventually, in *Part Two*, the rejection of Falstaff was played for pathos, and Richardson did emphasise those foreshadowings of his downfall that he could perform himself (his trembling 'do not bid me remember mine end' to Doll Tearsheet in *Part Two* attained a kind of cultural fame). What did not happen in this production of *Part One*, however, was a shift of control to Prince Hal as early as the tavern scene. It remained for the 1951 Stratford production, with Richard Burton as Hal, to bring that about.

* * *

1 Henry IV is not an attractive play for actresses. The female roles are slight and, in most of the big moments, invisible. Margaret Leighton as Lady Percy received attention because she held her own in Olivier's determination to portray the romantic elegance in their relationship. Later productions would turn this couple's first scene into sexy rough-and-tumble, but Leighton and Olivier were sexy without the need for acrobatics. Mistress Quickly does not seem enough of a part for Sybil Thorndike, who was ignored in most reviews, although part of her tremendous achievement in the theatre was the ability to care for something modest to the point of being just about perfect in it. Still, in *1 Henry IV*, the actresses were up against an unyielding text – there is not much for the women here. 'This is a play which all men admire, and most women dislike', wrote Elizabeth Inchbald in 1817 (Hemingway, p. 395), and I am not certain that any subsequent production has done much to change that.

The Old Vic prompt-book does show one nice bit of emphasis for the women, however. After the first verse of Lady Mortimer's Welsh song in Act III, the men delivered the concluding lines of the scene and went off to their non-musical business of indentures and rebellion. Lady Percy exited with Hotspur, as the text indicates she should, but Lady Mortimer (Diana Maddox) remained on stage alone, moved to a window, and sang a second verse of the Welsh song more or less to herself. Letting the music outlast the masculine business was a fine touch. Then Lady Percy returned to the stage and crossed to Lady Mortimer, joining her at the window in a silent gesture of sympathy. They must have been sharing a quality which men of battle do not regard closely.

This ending was not entirely orginal with Burrell's production (J. C. Trewin recalled a similar staging at Stratford in the 1930s – Beauman, *The Royal Shakespeare Company*, p. 89), but among the Old Vic company in 1945 it must have had some recent echoes. The Old Vic production of *Uncle Vanya* of the season before, which would be revived after *Henry IV* and the other new plays were established in 1945, would have had a similar scene. At the end of Act II in *Uncle Vanya*, two women, Sonia and Elena, share a moment of understanding over the hope that they could play some music in this dour household. The hope is dashed by the Professor, Elena's aged husband, who will not allow this kind of noise. One supposes that the similarity of scene endings must have been apparent to Margaret Leighton – the episode in *1 Henry IV* attaining what was denied in the Uncle Vanya episode, an exchange of female sympathy – for Leighton was Lady Percy in one and Elena in the other.

In real life, the men were talking business and laying plans. Behind this Old Vic production lay a hope for the future of the English theatre. For more than a century, plans for a National Theatre had been advanced, negotiated, abandoned, and resurrected. Three generations of advocates and potential donors were now in the grave. The war should have dealt the final blow to hopes for the National. It did deal the final blow to a South Kensington project for the new theatre, which had seemed ready to take shape in the late 1930s (Elsom and Tomalin, pp. 70-86).

Yet some had felt for years that the Old Vic already was something of a National Theatre, and the post-war success of the Olivier–Richardson–Burrell company raised hopes of formalising that impression. The Old Vic itself, before it was damaged in the air-raids, had been a theatre for the common people, and that tradition had not entirely been lost at the New in 1945. The Richardson–Olivier–Burrell productions were great popular successes. Half the seats at the New were priced from 1*s* 6*d* to 4*s* 6*d*, the price of ten to forty cigarettes (O'Conner, p. 135). Hundreds of people hired stools and queued on opening night in September, and on closing night in May, St Martin's Lane was blocked for an hour as 2,500 fans shouted for the stars, who made farewell remarks from the roof of a taxi (O'Conner, p. 129). But a gradual change in the direction of wealth had been occurring at the Old Vic since the 1930s, with productions becoming more expensive and the higher ticket prices steadily rising, and the *Henry IV* productions at the New, with their stars and their end-of-the-war importance, belonged to the new trend. The audiences may have been crowded with ordinary people, but they were headed by wealth, power, and glamour – elements from which a National Theatre can finally be made, despite the idealism that always hovers over such ventures with claims that the common people must be served. The Queen Mother, along with the Princesses Elizabeth and Margaret, attended *1 Henry IV* in November. Mrs Churchill was there on opening night, in September, along with the Earl of Lytton, Viscount Esher, Lord Hambledon, Sir Kenneth Clark, John Gielgud, Deborah Kerr, and Bea Lillie (Mr Churchill, the papers explained, was still in the south of France, concluding the war). When the production went to New York in May of the following year, Andrei Gromyko, Ingrid Bergman, Paulette Goddard, Gene Kelly, Olivia de Havilland, Lana Turner, Alfred Gwynne Vanderbilt, Jose Ferrer, and Ruth Gordon were recognised in the first-night audience.

Celebrities in the audience, celebrities on the stage – while they were all playing their roles, negotiations were growing serious behind the scenes. On 28 January 1946 the Old Vic and the Shakespeare Memorial National Theatre – rivals for years over the question of where a National Theatre should take root – held a joint press conference and announced that they would form an amalgamation to bring the long-cherished dream to actuality. It was understood that Old Vic actors would form the nucleus of the National company. The prestige of Olivier and Richardson, the administrative and directorial skill of Burrell, the depth and experience of the rest of the company – all these would combine to achieve what all the previous generations of prestige, skill, and experience had found impossible. Post-war euphoria helped build confidence in the venture, which seemed to be part of the new age. The Labour-controlled London County Council would develop plans for a new theatre on the South Bank. A National Theatre founded on the achievements of the Old Vic company would be the 'first artistic venture of our new, young, educated democracy', Viscount Esher said at the joint press conference (Elsom and

[32]

Tomalin, p. 85). But the connections between these elements were no more secure than the notion that somehow Olivier and Richardson could be linked to the interests of democratic social-ism. The promise of the Labour victory was shattered by the shortages, strikes, and hard winters of the next few years, and in the smaller world of culture, the heyday of the Olivier–Richardson–Burrell Old Vic was coming to an end. Olivier and Richardson grew busy with overseas tours and film commitments. Burrell was left at home to manage a company from which some of the veterans, like Harcourt Williams, had departed. It was decided that the contracts of the triumvirate could not be renewed, and the news was broken by the same Lord Esher who had thought the Old Vic could lead the new democratic order. Olivier got his cable in Australia, Richardson his in Hollywood (Elsom and Tomalin, pp. 87-96).

In the very long run – for that is what it took for the National to come into being – one can see bits of the hoped-for connection with the Old Vic: when the National was finally established in 1963, Olivier was its artistic director and the company was housed at the Old Vic itself for a decade before the new theatre complex on the South Bank was built. (One of the first plays done for the National at the Old Vic was a production of *Uncle Vanya* which had origi-nated a year earlier at Chichester. Olivier played Astrov and Sybil Thorndike played the old nurse Marina – the same roles they had played in the 1944 Old Vic production. Either in the mid-1940s or in the mid-1960s, then, perhaps in both, three generations of Lon-don theatregoers could have seen these two, Thorndike and Olivier, open Chekhov's play on the simplest gesture: 'Have a cup of tea, my dear.' It was a superb moment.)

One venture never undertaken at the National, however, is the one undertaken in 1945, when *1 Henry IV* opened the Old Vic sea-son that was supposed to cement the future. The National has never done Shakespeare's histories extensively. With great success have they have done the comedies and tragedies, but apart from the star turn, such as John Wood's in *Richard III*, the histories have not figured importantly at the National Theatre.

That is largely because the histories have been taken up and reconceived by other companies. No longer is *1 Henry IV* primarily seen as a vehicle for star performances in the roles of Falstaff and Hotspur. The most important productions now place the two parts of Henry IV into a context of other histories, and the format is the large-scale cycle, sometimes covering an entire week of performances. Ensemble work has taken precedence over the star performance. This change of emphasis originated in England's other long-standing classical theatre, the Shakespeare Memorial Theatre in Stratford-upon-Avon, where cycles were mounted in 1951, again in 1964, and yet again in 1975, 1982, and 1989, each approaching the plays from a different interpretative angle. In 1986 a new troupe called the English Shakespeare Company then produced another interpretation of the histories, startling to many, in their history cycle. Modern attitudes towards *1 Henry IV* have mainly been shaped by these large-scale productions, which will occupy much of the rest of this book.

I

II

III

IV

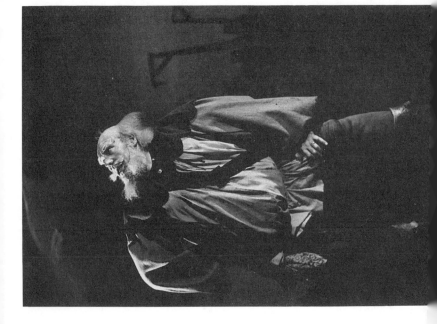

CHAPTER III

1951. The Shakespeare Memorial Theatre: Anthony Quayle

The year 1951 was that of the Festival of Britain, a nation-wide demonstration that post-war difficulties were over and England was entering the second half of the century on confident footing. This was not a new theme, and it will be recalled that the Old Vic was proving something like this with the the Olivier–Richardson–Burrell company at the end of the war. Some lessons have to be repeated, especially when events show they are not exactly based on truth. England's immediate post-war confidence ran aground owing to economic and natural hardships over which the theatre had no control – and then the Old Vic artistic directors were given the sack as well. Now another effort was to be made, and again the Shakespeare histories were called upon, this time at England's other classical theatre, the Shakespeare Memorial Theatre in Stratford-upon-Avon. Under the direction of Anthony Quayle, the 1951 Stratford season was largely given over to a *cycle* of the histories, four plays in series, running from *Richard II* through the two parts of *Henry IV* to *Henry V*.

These had been regarded as different kinds of plays in the theatre, and as vehicles for different kinds of leading actors. *Richard II* was pathos and tragedy: Gielgud came to mind. *Henry V* was martial and heroic: Olivier came to mind. Whether *1 Henry IV* was performed in isolation or in tandem with *Part Two*, comic interest focused on Falstaff and sentimental interest on Hotspur: since

1945, Richardson and Olivier came to mind. At Stratford in 1951 Anthony Quayle sought to prove something quite different: that the four plays were united by a single vision of English history and that one was not complete without the context of the other three. His method of demonstration was to stage the four plays on a single set and with a single company, the actors retaining those roles that carried over from one play to another.

The inspiration for this venture had a scholarly tinge. The idea of a Shakespearian historical cycle had been put into circulation during the war, especially by E. M. W. Tillyard's *Shakespeare's History Plays*. Tillyard's book was itself an act of faith in the war-time survival of English culture that was now to be celebrated by the Festival of Britain. According to Tillyard, Shakespeare conceived of his history plays – not just the four that Stratford would stage, but the eight plays that cover English chronicle material from the reign of Richard II through that of Richard III – as a vast cycle in which the central figure of the entire epic was England itself, an England shaped by principles of monarchy, genealogy, and order which it was a sin to disrupt. This book has fallen into disfavour today, when it has become the scholarly fashion to deride Tillyard for what he certainly did – read his own conservative ideology into the plays. But if scholarship gains from attending to its own period as well as to the period of its historical subject, Tillyard's study has a political range and cohesiveness that cannot be found in most of the careers that have been advanced by attacking it. Now that it can be read historically itself, it can be recognised as a profound wartime book, in which the discovery that England was the hero of the history plays was blended with the experience of readers for whom the survival of the nation was a crucial issue.

That Anthony Quayle read Tillyard has never been supposed, nor need it be. By the time Quayle conceived of the history cycle the Tillyard argument was in the air. It was part of the post-war Shakespeare scene whether one read it or not. Shakespeare was being used for nationalistic purposes, and the Tillyard thesis – that Shakespeare was a far-sighted designer of mighty structures – matched the image that the managers of British affairs wanted to project for their own efforts. When Tillyard's book was reviewed in the *TLS* in 1945, an editorial ran opposite the review and showed plainly what was at stake: 'the greatest English poet shall not be set down for a haphazard fluker, but known for a high and strenuous intellectual worker, rich in knowledge and firm in far-seeking purpose' – this as an aid toward overcoming 'the English reputation for blundering into success' (*TLS*, 6 January 1945, p. 7). Two months later the *TLS* carried a letter comparing the Shakespeare history plays to Wagner's Ring Cycle, a comparison that Tillyard had already made, and shaming Stratford for being a holiday resort instead of an English Bayreuth (*TLS*, 24 March 1945).

In 1945 the Stratford operation *was* a bit like a holiday resort, but by the time the history cycle opened in 1951, Quayle and his predecessor Barry Jackson had turned the Memorial Theatre into a respected and influential organisation. The Stratford system before the tenures of Jackson and Quayle was to stage a huge programme of ten plays each summer by retaining the veterans who had played Shakespeare for years, were fond of repeating their successful routines, and knew the Stratford theatre as they knew their sitting rooms. A company organised around such a nucleus could re-hearse five or six of the summer's plays in the spring, then kick off the season with a solid week of opening nights. No subsequent repertory company in England has been able to operate at such a pace, but the price to be paid for this system was the timid repetitiveness that Londoners like to call provincialism. The provincial theatre in England is actually a lively source of talent London could not do without, but in this case the pejorative was accurate. The theatre world was changing and was passing Stratford by. Seasoned Shakespearian actors were becoming known from one end of the town to the other, just when the new talent in England was gaining international fame through films and tours of London stage productions. Olivier, Richardson, John Gielgud, Alec Guinness, Michael Redgrave, Edith Evans, Vivien Leigh, Sybil Thorndike – there were stars in the English theatre during the 1940s; but while they were making their fame in film, in West End theatres, and on tour, the Stratford company was counting on Roy Byford and Randle Ayrton to give long-familiar performances. Let it not be thought that these were second-rate actors. They were top-flight Shakespeare professionals. Veteran theatregoers still live who insist that Byford and Ayrton have never been surpassed in some of their performances. But a shift had occurred in the acting profession with the development of film and stage industries that could reach international audiences, and the change was not taking hold in Stratford.

Barry Jackson, who became artistic director in 1946, cleared out

[37]

the long-term actors and the long-term employees, gave up the week of opening nights and the ten-play repertory, allowed each play a full month's rehearsal, and brought in new directors and new actors. He did not bring in the stars. That would be Quayle's doing. Jackson hired young actors and directors who showed abundant talent early – some would succeed, some would disappear. Among the former were Peter Brook and Paul Scofield. When Jackson left in 1948, Quayle took charge and sought leading actors for the major roles. But he also continued Jackson's precedent of hiring impressive young performers, retained Brook and Scofield from the Jackson regime, and added talented stage designers. Within a few years he had established a company that could rival anything London had to offer. Some said it now surpassed the Old Vic.

For the 1951 cycle of histories, Quayle assembled a large company. *1 Henry IV* had a cast of forty-six: twenty-nine for speaking roles and, luxuriantly, seventeen supernumeraries. These ample numbers allowed the retention of the Carriers' scene (II. i) and the colloquy between the Archbishop and Sir Michael (IV. iv), the two episodes normally cut from earlier productions. (The Old Vic production of 1945, which cut the two episodes and doubled more heavily, had a cast of twenty-seven, of whom twenty covered the speaking roles.) It may be noted that Quayle insisted on running the Stratford operation without subsidy. At the head of the 1951 company, Michael Redgrave was brought in to play Richard II and to follow that with Hotspur in *1 Henry IV*. Quayle himself played Falstaff, and an experienced actor of great power and intelligence, Harry Andrews, was Henry IV. This was one of the roles that changed most in the cycle format, for the now fatherly king of *Henry IV* was seen to be also the usurping king of *Richard II* and thus the source of the internal disruption that followed in the realm. In his performances across three plays, Andrews showed the King's degeneration from brisk ambition to careworn guilt – a portrayal that must have been new to everyone in the audience. But the stroke of casting that made the greatest difference at Stratford concerned Prince Hal/Henry V, which became the major role in the cycle format (and is, in fact, the longest Shakespearian role in its full extent across three plays). For this central assignment, Quayle hired a young Welsh actor who was unknown in most theatre circles, Richard Burton.

Setting an unknown as Hal against Redgrave's Hotspur might seem like the Old Vic casting described in the previous chapter, wherein a little-known actor had trouble contending with Olivier. But Quayle knew what he was looking for. He had heard that this young actor had given some startling performances as an undergraduate at Oxford and was now acting with Gielgud in London. The newcomer was said to be magnetic, the kind of actor from whom audiences could not take their eyes. Quayle saw him in Christopher Fry's *Boy with a Cart* and knew that here was a risk worth taking. An actor who demands to be seen and who surprises everyone with his talent would be exactly right for the Prince who suddenly rises to fame himself.

* * *

The way to stage a cycle is to rehearse all four plays at once and open them on successive first nights – a return, in effect, to the old Stratford system of opening a play each night. Quayle sought to do that, but the intensive rehearsal period could not be financed, and finally the four plays were opened at monthly intervals. As a result, the initial reviews tended to judge each play according to the old standards of isolated production. *Richard II*, the first to open, was studied for Michael Redgrave's performance in the title role, which some found to be lacking in pathos after Gielgud. The role in *Richard II* that mattered most for the cycle, the Bolingbroke of Harry Andrews, received secondary attention. In the two plays on Henry IV, Andrews' superb performance as the King could not be missed, and Burton's startling interpretation of Hal insured that the shift of emphasis to the royal father and son was well understood, but the older attitudes still surfaced when Quayle's Falstaff was felt to be too cold and unlovable. 'It makes one think, but it does not make one merry', as the *Manchester Guardian* said (quoted in Wilson and Worsley, p. 67). What Quayle's interpretation was designed to make one think *about* – the viciousness behind the comic in Falstaff, and the need for his ultimate rejection – rather passed unnoticed at first. And even Burton, whose Hal was rightly judged from the beginning, was thought to fall short of the Olivier-dominated 'heroic' mode for *Henry V*.

Thus the Stratford cycle had to win its way slowly. Tanya Moiseiwitsch's set, which in the long run was instrumental in gaining the cycle's effect of unity, was puzzling at first. She had the bold idea of building a virtual Elizabethan stage within the Stratford proscenium and using it for every scene in the four plays. She designed a framework of unvarnished timber, its downstage area set with wooden tables and chairs suggestive of a tavern but usable in any location. To one side stood a pavilion with a throne, which was lighted by itself at the beginning of each play. There was a gallery to the rear, reached by stairs on either side, and the space beneath the gallery could either be closed off by two doors to suggest an interior or be opened to the cyclorama for a vista. The large Stratford stage was transformed into a closely defined series of acting spaces into which the chronological sprawl of the four plays had to be fitted. This articulation of vast narrative in precise and repeated spaces created the effect of Elizabethan staging.

But at first some in the audience did not see how it worked. One reviewer thought the set resembled a 'railway-goods lift' (quoted in Findlater, *Michael Redgrave*, p. 102), and another thought it was a lobby between apartments (quoted in Wilson and Worsley, p. 54). A fundamental incongruity was unavoidable: setting a quasi-Elizabethan stage into the proscenium of the Stratford Memorial Theatre tries to combine two fundamentally different ideas of the disposition between stage and audience. The basic idea of the original Elizabethan theatre was to thrust its stage into the midst of spectators and insist on immediate contact between actor and audience. The Stratford stage is a cavern into which audiences peer from a distance (an effect in part ameliorated by building out the apron stage and redesigning the auditorium just before the 1951 season – but still, Stratford insistently separates audience from actor). The Moiseiwitsch set was bravely Elizabethan, but it necessarily sat back from the audience and held the action at the accustomed distance of realism. That the main acting space could serve for a court scene at one moment and a tavern scene at the next seemed confusing to some, even though the court scenes were signalled by lighting up the throne pavilion. When in a court scene King Henry perched on one of the tables, the reviewer for the *Evening Standard* wondered how he had got into the tavern (4 April 1951). The critic for *The Birmingham Post* said 'any sense of royal occasion is blunted when affairs of State are conducted on the stairs' (4 April 1951). Within a decade, modern thrust stages at Stratford, Ontario, at Chichester, and at the Guthrie Theatre in Minneapolis would make the conventions of non-illusionistic stage spaces that Moiseiwitsch was counting on at the Memorial Theatre in 1951 common and widely practised (she designed the thrust stage in Ontario herself), but it was not until the entire cycle was mounted two-thirds of the way through the season that her timber-framed Elizabethan set was generally appreciated (Wilson and Worsley, pp. 53-4).

Of the four plays, *1 Henry IV* fared best from opening night. The latter two parts of the cycle had yet to be staged, but those in the audience who had seen *Richard II* were in position, for the first time in memory, to give up the assumption that these are separate plays and to understand the second one in terms of the first. When King Henry summons his prodigal son to court and upbraids him for acting like Richard II in days gone by, for example, spectators who had seen *Richard II* for themselves would now realise that the King is wide of the mark:

> The skipping King, he ambled up and down
> With shallow jesters and rash bavin wits,
> Soon kindled and soon burnt; carded his state,
> Mingled his royalty with cap'ring fools,
> Had his great name profaned with their scorns,
> And gave his countenance, against his name,
> To laugh at gibing boys and stand the push
> Of every beardless vain comparative;
> Grew a companion to the common streets,
> Enfeoffed himself to popularity,
> That, being daily swallowed by men's eyes,
> They surfeited with honey and began
> To loathe the taste of sweetness ... (III. ii. 60-72)

This is not an apt description of Shakespeare's Richard II. King Henry is seizing on popular legends about the 'skipping King' in order to gain the comparison he needs to rebuke his son in politically significant terms, but spectators who saw Redgrave play Richard II the night before would know that the comparison is wrenched. They would also know that Redgrave was playing Hotspur tonight, a piece of casting that shows up the King's anxieties: wanting Hal to be more like Hotspur but not at all like Richard II sounds like a father under strain if Hotspur and Richard II are played by one performer (Redgrave looked different, Redgrave sounded different, but there is no escaping it, he was the same). If *1 Henry IV* is staged by itself, the King's account quoted above seems merely authoritative, but the combination of plays allows for fresh possibilities of cross-over reasoning.

And the raising of fresh possibilities was felt in this *1 Henry IV*. One read the present performance back against the previous one, and read it forward too, with expectation of what might follow in the later *Henrys*. T. C. Worsley caught this questioning spirit in the

New Statesman: it is a help 'to have the events of *Richard II* so alive in our memories, and, no less, we have to look forward to the events that are coming .... One may almost see the producer's mind ranging forwards and backwards from this point' (quoted in Wilson and Worsley, p. 66). And the forward-looking question to be asked of this young Prince of Wales, being so roundly misunderstood by his father in the scene of royal rebuke, suffering a comparison with Richard II that simply does not hold up to experience – the question to be asked, if further plays lie ahead, is how can he develop into the hero-king, Henry V?

* * *

In 1951, that was really a question about Richard Burton. Quayle's decision to cast him as Prince Hal and thus to set him against Redgrave's Hotspur brought the turning-point in the young actor's career. It did not matter to Burton that Hotspur had been the sentimental choice in this contest for generations. He had three plays ahead of him as Prince and King, his role central to each one of them, and he had the nerve to interpret that role in ways that no one had seen before. Prince Hal was supposed to be a roisterer and a boon companion who must learn to take kingship seriously – or at least he was *pretending* to be that way. But Burton's Hal was not even pretending. He was a troubled young man who stood apart from the Eastcheap crowd, eyeing them and already thinking ahead, uneasily, to the role he would eventually assume. It was a performance based on the soliloquy which ends Hal's first scene, in which he coldly predicts that he will cast aside Falstaff and the tavern crowd in order to make a great impression of reform before he becomes King:

> I know you all, and will awhile uphold
> The unyoked humour of your idleness.
> Yet herein will I imitate the sun,
> Who doth permit the base contagious clouds
> To smother up his beauty from the world,
> That, when he please again to be himself,
> Being wanted, he may be more wondered at
> By breaking through the foul and ugly mists
> Of vapours that did seem to strangle him. (I. ii. 183-91)

This had been a moment to get over quickly by most Hals, for it says that the good-natured prankster Prince of the same scene had been calculating his behaviour. The actor who wants Hal to be well liked tends to be brisk with the soliloquy, playing it straightfordwardly and letting it inform the audience without deepening the characterisation. Commentators had long recommended avoiding deep characterisation here. They sought to avoid what would look like a *hypocritical* Prince of Wales by arguing that the speech was not a true piece of characterisation at all, but a 'signal' of the action to follow, a merely conventional way of passing information to the audience (see quotes in Hemingway, pp. 48-9). Michael Warre's straightforward delivery of the surface of the speech in the Old Vic production was in keeping with this interpretation: the speech means exactly what it says, but it does not reveal the character at hand so much as it promises the action to follow.

Burton used the speech to reveal the character. His Hal had been calculating something from the moment he came on, holding himself a little remote from Falstaff and Poins even as he agreed to join their exploit, and he integrated the soliloquy with this studied and uneasy behaviour. I have suggested in the previous chapter that the soliloquy provides a rhetorical enlargement of Hal's role, the change from prose to verse and the change from dialogue to soliloquy both serving to broaden the range of the speaker's authority from the historical setting to the theatre itself. Burton neatly caught the shift to the theatre audience, but he was not interested in the rhetorical change from prose to verse. This Hal was speaking from one sub-text all the way through the scene. He was not at home with Falstaff and Poins. He was not at home with himself. He stood apart from the others earlier and, without moving, he stood apart from the audience when he addressed them. He did not change anything but the field of his vision when the soliloquy arose. He 'turned to watch Falstaff leave the stage; for a moment he stood looking after him; then his head moved slowly to regard the audience over his shoulder, and the speech followed, with a curious simplicity and tonelessness, and yet with a suggestion of strong emotion held in check' (David, 'Shakespeare's History Plays,' p. 136). Thus the audience was suddenly addressed, and yet there was no change in the speaker. He was no closer to the spectator than he was to Falstaff. He was a stranger all round, and he was on a quest that was largely interior no matter what he said about it.

In other words, this Hal had a gloomy sense of his destiny from the beginning, and the interpretation was projected forward in keeping with the design of the cycle. Exactly what that destiny was remained mysterious. By the time *Henry V* reached the Stratford stage, Burton was being criticised for falling short of heroic royalty, but it is not clear that his Hal was suffering from anxieties that could be allayed by something so worldly as a crown. His quest struck several reviewers as being tinged with a virtually religious mystery (although the possibility should not be dismissed that here is a case of a Welshman putting one over on the English). Certainly no Hal had ever been reviewed in the terms Harold Hobson bestowed on this performance, for Hobson is describing transcendence:

> This production offers what must be one of the rarest of theatrical experiences: namely, a performance in a principal part which, in the light of the text and the received notions of the author's intentions, cannot be accorded even the moderate praise of being called good, yet which gives the deep and ordered emotional release that is among the actual marks of greatness. [The greatness] is in the bone and sinew of the performance, and is as evident in the actor's stillness when other players are speaking as when he is sailing full flood .... Mr. Burton looked like a man who had had a private vision of the Holy Grail, and was as determined to say nothing about it as he was incapable of forgetting it .... Mr. Burton offers a young knight keeping a long vigil in the cathedral of his own mind. (*Sunday Times*, 8 April 1951)

Lest this be thought to be only one person's opinion, here is independent witness from Kenneth Tynan:

> His playing of Prince Hal ... turned interested speculation to awe as soon as he started to speak: in the first intermission the local critics stood agape in the lobbies ... His Prince Hal is never a roaring boy: he sits hunched or sprawled, with dark unwinking eyes: he hopes to be amused by his bully companions, but the eyes constantly muse beyond them into the time when he must steady himself for the crown. 'He brings his cathedral with him,' said one dazed member of the company. (Quoted in Bragg, p. 74)

With expectations like these, it is little wonder that Henry V, who merely conquers France and takes a bride, was a bit of a disappointment.

* * *

The more famous actors received credit, some of it from themselves, for the adjustments they made to the phenomenon of Burton. Lecturing to some drama students the following year, Redgrave recalled holding back his performance as Hotspur so as 'to restore Prince Hal to his proper status as the hero' (*The Actor's Ways and Means*, p. 44). His Hotspur was energetic and amusing, but never the sentimental magnet Olivier had made of the part. He was rowdy, funny, and dangerous. 'I felt that the clue to his character,' Redgrave wrote years later, 'lay in the fact that he was a rough, down-to-earth countryman, who was ignorant in the ways of the court and proud of it' (Sales, p. 112). 'A pelting, tumultuous study', J. C. Trewin called his performance (*The Lady*, 19 April 1951). This Hotspur 'is always on the edge of action, even in repose, perpetually balanced up on the balls of his feet ready to spring, all of a straight supple piece', said T. C. Worsley (*The New Statesman*, 21 April 1951).

His boisterousness (and Barbara Jefford's, as Lady Percy) can be gathered from the notes of the prompt-book at the Shakespeare Centre Library in Stratford. The first scene between Hotspur and Lady Percy calls for a comic battle between the two from the beginning: they 'struggle at end of table', 'Hotspur made to sit on table by Lady P', he 'sits Lady P on his knee', then 'dumps her on table'. They are to be kissing by the end of all this. Such rough-and-tumble sexiness has now become standard in this scene, although it now gives a more favourable impression. When John Price and Jen Stoller wrestled and tumbled with one another in the 1986 English Shakespeare Production, they were engagingly frank and physical with one another (in contrast to Michael Pennington's Hal, who tried to avoid physical contact with anyone). But Redgrave and Jefford made the audience worry about the 'violence' of their sexuality, which would not be found among better-behaved people at Court: using 'a tone of violence which you would never find at the Court, [Lady Percy] upbraids him, and with the same kind of violence he pushes her away, not gently rebuffing but violently rejecting what are in effect violent sexual overtones' (Wilson and Worsley, p. 45).

As for the stammer, Redgrave refused to have one. Instead he went to the pubs and manor houses of Northumberland in search of a burred 'R' two months before opening ('Hotspur Looks for a Burr in the Bar', *Newcastle Evening Chronicle*, 12 February 1951), and found an accent that could be ignored no more easily than it could be placed. Londoners thought it Scots, the Scots thought it Northumbrian, and Northumberland in the play must have thought it queer, for it did not sound at all like him. The effect was to make Hotspur a displaced Northerner, a stranger even to his own faction, 'a lawless adventurer who might well prove a danger to the commonwealth' (Findlater, *Michael Redgrave*, p. 107).

Quayle's Falstaff sacrificed some of the role's popularity in order to give an underlying feeling of viciousness to the comedy. His make-up, for example, was at first the strangest ever seen on a Falstaff (Quayle toned it down after the reviews came out). The intention was to give a metallic, overworked aspect to the lovable rogue everyone expected to see, so that the humour would have to fight its way across an image of artifice. The initial reviews reflected some consternation over this effort, which for one critic made Quayle look like 'a cross between an aged circus clown and a Halloween turnip' (*Daily Express*, 4 April 1951). The *Times* review was shrewd about the purpose behind Quayle's appearance:

> The Falstaff of Mr. Anthony Quayle is more than half aware that his standing with the Prince is in doubt. This awareness has affected his geniality, for Mr. Quayle is strictly loyal to the Festival's historical design. His make-up is rather grotesque than laughable; he speaks the jests with metallic precision; and his smile when it appears is a painted smile. This tuned-down Falstaff has the supreme merit of suiting the production, and no one but a very good actor could bring it off half so well. (Quoted in Wilson and Worsley, pp. 66-7)

Confronted with Burton's sullen, withdrawn Hal, this Falstaff had to work overtime in order to create the fun and fellowship that are traditionally supposed to be spontaneous between the pair. In their first scene, when they were supposed to be joking about the thievery that will be possible once Hal becomes king, Falstaff had to rise to higher and higher extravagances, eyeing Hal all the time, before he could get a response. 'Let us be Diana's foresters', was met with a stare (I. ii. 24). 'Gentlemen of the shade' was raised a pitch higher. Still, the stare. Then, with some cooing and strutting, the perfect phrase 'Minions of the moon' got his laugh at last, an effect aided by cutting the rest of Falstaff's speech and the first lines of Hal's response (Wilson and Worsley, p. 49. The cut is marked in the prompt-book).

The tension between Falstaff and Hal can be seen most clearly in Quayle's handling of the first tavern scene. When the trap was sprung, and Hal and Poins told Falstaff that they were the intruders he was claiming to have outfought, Quayle seemed almost dangerous:

> For a moment he would stand between them like a cornered rat, head settled into hunched shoulders and his body pinched and withdrawn,

while beneath bushy brows his eyes shifted from one to the other of his captors, measuring, calculating, seeking a way out. Then suddenly the idea would come, his whole person would expand, and he would overwhelm them with a tidal wave of confidence and explanations. (David, 'Shakespeare's History Plays,' p. 136)

In the play-acting scene that followed, Burton turned usually jovial moments into a deadly battle. His 'there is a devil haunts thee in the likeness of an old fat man' (II. iv. 431) was unsmiling and chilling. The tavern onlookers began to lose their laughter at this point. The fun of seeing Falstaff parody the Prince of Wales to his face was over, and the crowd was not sure what would follow. Hal's list of epithets for Falstaff – 'that trunk of humours, that bolting-hutch of beastliness, that swoll'n parcel of dropsies' (II. iv. 433-5) – seemed to restore the tone of outrageous joking, and the prompt-book calls for the crowd to cheer at 'roasted Manningtree ox', but Burton's recital of vices continued too long and came across too deliberately, and the laughter grew uneasy again. 'Wherein is he good, but to taste sack and drink it? Wherein neat and cleanly, but to carve a capon and eat it? Wherein cunning but in craft? Wherein crafty but in villainy?' – the prompt-book marks a pause after each of the 'wherein' clauses, making each into a separate condemnation, and the exchange of

Fal. My lord, the man I know.
Prin. I know thou dost.

caused 'a moment's queer, horrid silence' in the crowd (Wilson and Worsley, p. 50).

Falstaff's recovery – the long speech ending with 'banish plump Jack, and banish all the world' – drew the crowd back to his side, the side of comedy. The prompt-book calls for a 'loud cheer' as he reaches his crescendo. Then comes a controversial moment. Hal's response to 'banish plump Jack, and banish all the world' has now become a moment of high significance in modern productions, as though the line 'I do, I will' is his discovery of what he will eventually do to Falstaff, or his prediction of what he will do, or both. The days of innocence when the line could be tossed away with the fling of a cushion, as was done in the Old Vic production, are over. Now the knocking at the door (which ends the play-acting, for the sheriff is looking for Falstaff) has to be delayed a minute while Hal looks his Falstaff in the eye and gives 'I do, I will' a measured reading which the old man hears as a foreshadowing of his rejection. As T.

F. Wharton says, 'It is an arresting, an unsettling theatrical moment. The most obvious way of producing it in the theatre is to allow it to stop the show; to stop the actors in their tracks, reduce everything to silence, broken only by the knocking at the door' (Wharton, p. 41).

Burton seems to have been responsible for this interpretation, but exactly when he introduced it is difficult to say. The interpretation certainly fits with Burton's conception of a far-sighted and melancholy Hal, and one would assume that the new reading was in place early. The young actor's mentor, Philip Burton, says in an unpublished manuscript that he suggested the serious reading in 1951, despite Quayle's dismay at the loss of comedy in the play-acting scene overall (quoted in Bragg, p. 72). Quayle himself did not accede to the view that he was plumping for more comedy, but the prompt-book makes it evident that the weighted reading of the line was not originally intended. It marks no pause in connection with 'I do, I will.' More significantly, it shows that the knocking at the door, with plenty of business – Francis entering, Peto and Gadshill changing position – came directly after the loud cheer on Falstaff's 'banish all the world'. This is the older timing of the scene's ending, with Hal's line becoming part of the shuffle. If Philip Burton is correct, it would appear that Quayle originally saw nothing special in the line and intended to end the scene in the traditional way (as the prompt-book indicates) only to have Burton turn the scene around on 'I do, I will' sometime during rehearsals or the run. Two later productions in which Quayle played Falstaff (without Burton) – a 1964 recording for Caedmon and the 1979 BBC television version – both employ the weighted reading.

If the tavern scene showed the colder, more calculating side of Burton's Hal, his victory over Hotspur at Shrewsbury revealed signs of the maturity and humanity that would be developed in Henry V. His desire to engage Hotspur in single combat, expressed to his father at V. i. 100, was the beginning of the strong public Hal. The duel itself carried this motif further: here was no 'playboy turned swordsman', but 'the future Henry of Agincourt, emerging from the clouds of dissipation' (*Observer*, 7 April 1951). And a moment later, when he thought Falstaff lay dead before him, Burton's farewell lifted the repressions which had obscured his affection before, and evident was 'the common touch, the warm humanity, which is a keynote of true greatness' (*Birmingham News*, 7 April 1951). It is, of course, a moment when the rejection of Falstaff no longer seems necessary. It looks like the old man is dead. With the need for calculation out of the way, Hal's true feelings come to the surface. There is no sentimentality in the lines, but Burton recognised that Hal's oddly jocular remarks – 'could not all this flesh keep in a little life?' (V. iv. 101-2) – were different from the ugly string of epithets he had unleashed at the Boar's Head. This was now irony in the face of sorrow, and a Hal of deeper feeling was becoming apparent.

* * *

As in the 1945 Old Vic production, two intervals were taken, one after each of the tavern scenes. An advantage of this spacing is that it allowed expansive treatment of the three scenes which thus formed the middle section: the Welsh scene, which has Lady Mortimer's song, the scene of royal rebuke in which Hal confronts his father for the first time, and the second tavern scene, in which Hal announces that war is afoot and Falstaff receives his command. This was a short 'act' in any event, and the three scenes needed to be given their full measure.

The Welsh scene benefited most. I have described the coda by which the Old Vic production brought Lady Percy back on the second verse of Lady Mortimer's song, so that the women had a moment together. At Stratford in 1951, this special touch for the actresses was not employed. The scene gained its momentum instead from its Welsh authenticity. It was propelled by one of the Welshmen in the company – not Burton this time, but Hugh Griffith, who played such a glowering, forceful Glendower that one was prepared to believe him about raising spirits from the vasty deep. Griffith was also responsible for writing out the Welsh speeches of Lady Mortimer (played by Sybil Williams, Burton's wife – this was a very Welsh production). Here is one description of the results:

> With admirable restraint the producer allowed this scene to take its own time and – as never before in my experience – it was given in full, with long and passionate speeches in Welsh for Glendower's daughter. For one listener, at least, there was no sense of flagging, but it might have been otherwise without Hugh Griffith's Glendower; no ranting pomposo, this, for all his occasional flamboyances, but the dangerous, enigmatical and compelling personality that alone can cast the spell the scene demands. (David, 'Shakespeare's History Plays,' p. 135)

It may be added that Griffith's Welsh text was preserved and used in the next Stratford production, in 1964, by which time Griffith himself had gone on to play Falstaff.

The rebuke scene was strengthened by the contrast in acting styles between Burton and Harry Andrews, who played the King. Andrews was as responsible as anyone for the success of the entire cycle, thanks to 'a concentrated vigour which brings tinglingly alive the man who is efficient enough to usurp a Kingdom but lacks the imagination to rule it' (*The Times*, quoted in Wilson and Worsley, p. 69). His King in *1 Henry IV* had aged suddenly from the usurper of *Richard II*, yet he could still rise to a memorable anger. Having dismissed Worcester at I. iii. 21, he turned to Northumberland with a controlled fury: 'You / were / about / to / speak' (Wilson and Worsley, pp. 70-1). Yet later in the same scene, on the short line to Hotspur, 'I tell thee' (I. iii. 115), he clutched his heart in pain: 'King has heart attack' reads the prompt-book. (Andrews was turning up elements of the role that later actors would find useful: the King's illness, for example, came in for further variations in Eric Porter's King Henry of 1964 and in Jon Finch's television performance for the BBC in 1979.) Andrews' performance in I. iii made one wonder if this King of anger and illness was liable to break down, but in the later rebuke scene, the King had these difficulties under control. His voice sprang to the rhetoric of the lines, in contrast to Burton's monotone. The father was alight with rich, angry language. The son endured this rebuke with gawky understatement, until his own anger broke out:

> I will redeem all this on Percy's head,
> And in the closing of some glorious day
> Be bold to tell you that I am your son ... (III. ii. 132-4)

Directing his anger at Percy allowed Burton to accept his father's challenge. The Stratford prompt-book has Burton kneeling at 'This in the name of God I promise here' (III. ii. 153), only to be raised and kissed on his forehead by his father at the end of the scene. This was a 1950s touch. The scene was not to be permitted such tenderness in later RSC productions.

Indeed, later versions had to take the 1951 production as a standard to be challenged – it was that good. A better *orthodox* version would be hard to imagine. Doing the play as part of a cycle allowed a political emphasis to replace the sentimentality of loss in which Olivier and Richardson had specialised at the Old Vic. Now Henry IV and Hal were the centre of attention much of the time, the towers that defined the entire vast structure. Kingship was the main issue – a guilt-ridden kingship in the case of the father, a troubled and ambitious kingship in the case of the son. The 'tragic' part of Richard II was just as much an actor's plum as ever, but it now came as a prologue to the primary story. Falstaff was still the aim of the Shakespearian comic actor, but this was now a Falstaff whose demanding role appears only in the middle plays of a cycle that depends on his rejection and passes on to show the successful career of the king who rejects him.

The 1951 production worked these ideas out fully and became the landmark production for later generations. As I have indicated in the Introduction, there is no hard evidence that Shakespeare planned these plays as a cycle, despite Tillyard's argument, but the Stratford season of 1951 virtually made the case that he should have. Staged on the inventive Moiseiwitsch set, given a wonderful boost by the surprising performance of Burton, *supplemented* by performers of the calibre of Redgrave, Quayle, Barbara Jefford, and Harry Andrews, the entire series of four plays unified by one conception – there was no way to imitate this production by repeating its interpretation, and there was also no way to ignore its achievement. From this time to the present, the cycle format has been Stratford's standard approach to *1 Henry IV*, in recognition of the 1951 accomplishment. What has been shown to occur within the cycle, however, is something vastly different indeed.

CHAPTER IV

1964. The Royal Shakespeare Company: Peter Hall

The Stratford cycle of 1951 seemed of epic scale in its own day, but it did not tell the whole story of Shakespeare's history plays. It took *Henry V* as its goal and stopping-point. Olivier's 1944 film had defined the hero of Agincourt as the summing-up of British motives and power, and post-war England seemed to find this a natural treatment of the Shakespearian vision. The 1951 cycle raised darker psychological questions about this hero's growth to power, but it ended with a *Henry V* that did not subvert the image Olivier had left. Richard Burton was criticised for not being sufficiently heroic in the role, but no one thought he was trying to portray an anti-hero. The Festival of Britain was not the place for looking beyond Henry V to see what Shakespeare's plays would show about the aftermath of his reign.

The aftermath is actually where Shakespeare started. Early in his career he wrote four connected plays on the reigns of Henry VI and Richard III. Only the last of these was at all well known in post-war Britain, and its most famous manifestion was another film by Olivier, his *Richard III*, which came out in 1955 and made no connection with his *Henry V*. The warrior-king was one matter, the intriguing tyrant was another. What bridges the gap between them in the Shakespeare canon is the three parts of *Henry VI*, but most people knew little about the three parts of *Henry VI*. Tillyard's book on *Shakespeare's History Plays* had claimed that the early plays were part of the overall Wagnerian design of the Shakespearian series running from *Richard II* to *Richard III*, but the theatre was for the most part content to reflect the cycle theory through the plays of established popularity, conclude them with the victory at Agincourt, and leave *Henry VI* to the scholars. There had been a production of the *Henry VI* plays in Birmingham in the 1950s, but for the most part they were thought to be Shakespeare's apprentice work, pieced together when he was collaborating with lesser writers.

So the Stratford productions of 1951 opened everyone's eyes to the Shakespeare history cycle without giving all the possible dimensions to the cycle. If Shakespeare conceived of a cycle of histories, then *Henry V* is not the conclusion of the story. It is the middle. And the unstaged *Henry VI* plays lie just ahead.

* * *

In 1963 the Royal Shakespeare Company, as the Stratford organisation was now known, turned the three parts of *Henry VI* into two plays, added *Richard III* to form a trilogy, and went on in the following year to do what Shakespeare did, reach back to the earlier chronicle material and produce *Richard II*, the two parts of *Henry IV*, and *Henry V*. Agincourt was now the middle of an astonishing cycle of seven plays covering Shakespeare's view of English history from Richard II to Richard III. It was possible to see all seven plays in succession, and many people did.

What had happened at Stratford between 1951 and 1964 – if one of the major stories of the English theatre can be boiled down to a name or two – is that the company came under the direction of Peter Hall, an extremely energetic and able administrator, who secured a major government subsidy, added a London base of operations at the Aldwych Theatre, launched a season of experimental plays at the Arts Theatre, and hired Peter Brook to direct another experiment, the 'Theatre of Cruelty', at the LAMDA studio theatre. Hall was bent on extending the range of the company in two directions – from Shakespeare to contemporary plays and from Stratford to London. He hired young actors and guaranteed them several years of work. He had them take voice lessons, acting lessons, fencing lessons, sonnet lessons. He consulted them, so it seemed, on important company decisions. His goal was the development of an ensemble style that would work for modern plays as well as for Shakespeare – and by 1963, only three years after he started, he and his cohorts had changed the character of English theatre.

[53]

The early histories, performed in 1963, made a large share of the difference. Hall's associate at the RSC, John Barton, had long thought the three parts of *Henry VI* should be staged, especially as he would rewrite them into a two-part play and join them to a touched-up *Richard III* to make a trilogy called *The Wars of the Roses*. The project appealed to Hall, among other reasons, because there is no star role in these plays except that of Richard III, and even Richard has to develop out of the lesser role of Gloucester in *3 Henry VI*. This would be excellent training ground for a young company. Many of the parts carry from one play to the next, allowing scope for the best actors to develop. Moreover, a three-play cycle without star performers would require a strong directorial conception to give narrative and visual unity to the sprawling chronicles – Hall was not of a mood or an age to hide his ambitions. And these histories, unlike the 1951 group, were bleakly anti-heroic, capable of making war seem devastating and inhuman. The younger theatregoers of 1963 did not share the end-of-war patriotism that had motivated the 1945 Old Vic productions of *Henry IV* and the 1951 Stratford series for the Festival of Britain. The sensibilities of the new audience were being shaped by Beckett, Osborne, Pinter, Brecht. This was not a crowd given to what they would have regarded as the sentiment and jingoism of the past, and Hall rightly sensed that they would lean toward the discovery that plays deemed inferior by the older generation were just the ticket for the 1960s.

The actors had to master two special techniques for these productions. They had to learn how to speak Shakespeare's early verse, which in the histories swells with the sort of formal vaunting and taunting that is fustian to modern ears. And they had to learn how to fight with medieval weapons so the violence that fills these plays would seem dangerous and convincing.

Hall solved the problem of the verse by the age-old theatrical idea of pretending that it was better than it appeared. The actors learned to cut through the fustian to the underlying clarity and form of the blank verse line. The pressure toward rhetorical strutting was resisted, and the impression of overblown writing miraculously disappeared. The language seemed connected to real political and personal motives – that is what an assertion of underlying clarity and form can do. As for the battle scenes, John Barton recognised that the realism of fighting is both dull to watch and dangerous to engage in, so he invented a theatrical system of battle, a 'technique of making everything *look* as dangerous as possible, while at the same time ensuring the maximum of safety' (Addenbrooke, p. 206). How this was actually done has not been recorded, but it can be reported from the audience perspective that sparks were flying into the auditorium from the clang and clash of broadswords, maces, and armour. If this was safe for the actors, so be it. One spark flying towards the audience is proof enough that *someone* is in danger, and that makes the battle real.

The Wars of the Roses opened at Stratford in the summer of 1963, proved immensely successful, and moved to the Aldwych later in the year. Virtually no one who cared about English theatre had seen the *Henry VI* plays before, and now no one could miss them. The young audiences who had been nourished on Pinter and Beckett were going to Shakespeare, especially on marathon Saturdays, when all three plays could be seen in one day. These were eye-opening productions, and with the rest of the histories being planned for a cycle of a size that had never been tried before (the occasion, in 1964, was the 400th anniversary of Shakespeare's birth), it was clear that neither Shakespeare's early histories nor the Royal Shakespeare Company would ever be the same again.

The two parts of *Henry IV*, along with *Richard II* and *Henry V*, belonged to the second instalment of the cycle a year later. The new productions were thus designed to fit into an established context. The destination of the cycle was already known: the unheroic power politics and brutality of the *Henry VI* plays and *Richard III*. The new productions being added in 1964 were under an extraordinary pressure to match the achievements of 1963. Tried and true approaches to the plays were not likely to answer the new demands. In 1945 Olivier and Richardson had specialised in the pathos of loss for Falstaff and Hotspur. In 1951 Quayle and Burton had aimed for the evolution of heroism in Hal and the need to reject Falstaff's licentiousness. Both of those productions had assumed that the greatness of the *Henry IV* plays lay in the depth of the characterisation. Now, however, the *Henry IV* plays would have to create a momentum that would carry through *Henry V* to the harsh portrayal of power politics in the *Wars of the Roses*. Character flattens a little under this pressure, and becomes liable to a narrative momentum under control of the director and the designer. The overall design of the cycle was primary, and this meant that the directorial team would dictate the main lines of interpretation.

[55]

Peter Hall saw the dominant image as a mechanism of power:

'Over the years I became more and more fascinated by the contortions of politicians and by the corrupting seductions experienced by anyone who wields power. ... I realized that the mechanism of power had not changed in centuries. We also were in the middle of a blood-soaked century. I was convinced that a presentation of one of the bloodiest and most hypocritical periods of history would teach many lessons about the present.' (Quoted in Addenbrooke, p. 127)

One reason for the success of the cycle was that the designer, John Bury, was able to turn this conception into visual terms. Bury saw the violence and power politics of the cycle as framed in steel:

It was a period of armour and a period of the sword: they were plays about warfare, about power, about danger. One spent one's time either in armour, or piercing someone's armour – or being pierced. ... We were trying to make a world: a dangerous world, a terrible world, in which all these happenings fit. (Quoted in Addenbrooke, p. 212)

The stage floor was plated steel. The acting space for all seven plays was defined by two huge triangle-based metal-plated walls, which could be turned to present different faces and shifted to form different angles. The scenes had their own configurations, but one knew the large units were the same no matter how they were placed. Try to make a dent in *this* system, the setting seemed to say.

No decoration graced these structures. There was no ornamentation – the dominant metallic textures were modified here and there by wood and cloth, and banners were used in the battle scenes, but austerity prevailed in the overall visual impression. Bury had learned his craft over fifteen years at Joan Littlewood's Theatre Workshop at Stratford East, where the lack of a budget for 'design' meant that each set had to be improvised out of the materials at hand and built on the stage. Having a budget at the RSC did not change his fundamental approach, and the metal, wood, and cloth of the history cycle, no matter what they really did cost, had the feel of having been riveted, or hammered, or sewn by people who lived in the world of these plays. The costumes and properties were similarly plain and rugged. Some browns made their appearance in the costumes and tavern scenes of *1 Henry IV* and became more prominent in the autumnal coloration given to Justice Shallow's orchard in *Part Two*, but something else was taking over as the cycle progressed into *Henry V* and *Henry VI* – the metal was becoming more and more pronounced, was rusting as the civil wars continued, and was being replaced by darker metal, as though something else was taking over. It was hard black enamel that was taking over, black enamel and black leather, in the totalitarian reign of Richard III.

This delineation of the acting space had an immense impact on the productions. As with the Moiseiwitsch setting for the four-play cycle at Stratford in 1951, the use of a single architectural design gave an impression of unity to the entire series of plays. Hall was quick to provide commentary on that unity, and it gives one pause to detect in some of his remarks in 1963 something very like the idea about order that lay behind Quayle's conception of the 1951 cycle: 'All Shakespeare's thinking, whether religious, political, or moral,' Hall said, 'is based on a complete acceptance of this concept of order. There is a just proportion in all things: man is above beast, king is above man, and God above king' (quoted in Dollimore and Sinfield, p. 160). In this system, revolution is anathema: it 'destroys the order and leads to destructive anarchy'. But Hall was not settling for this Tillyard-inspired thesis about order. His conception of order was joined to his metaphor of the 'power machine'. Each time the large units of the set swung into position, the unity of using the same set pieces for each play gave an image of order, but it was order operating by unseen control and giving its own interpretations. The objects looked as if they were made by people from the world of the play, but something more powerful had taken over. No one was moving these units. They just moved. The stage was itself a huge machine in productions which were said to be about the machine of power politics, and Hall's conservative notions about the primacy of 'order' were edged with the ironic and hopeless view that humanity is helpless before the operations of the power machine. As Alan Sinfield has pointed out, Hall's thinking was Tillyard merged with Jan Kott (Dollimore and Sinfield, pp. 160-4).

The *Henry IV* plays had to be fitted to this harsh and power-driven environment. Clearly the production would press towards the rejection of Falstaff at the moment of Henry V's coronation, just as the next play would press through the reign of Henry V to portray its degeneration into the baronial wars of the subsequent plays. But the *Henry IV* plays have elements that cannot be easily subsumed by narrative drive and the machinery of royal politics. The problem is most obvious with Falstaff, but it also can be seen in the activity of common life that fills out the Eastcheap and Gloucestershire scenes in these two plays, where tavern drawers,

[57]

prostitutes, roaring boys, out-at-elbow aristocrats, farmers, and tailors all have personalities to assert and scenes to perform, before the machine can use them for its own purposes. The 1964 production, like the l951 version before it, had a large company (thirty performers for speaking roles, fifteen supernumeraries) and was able to fill out the larger scenes with convincing crowds.

In a bold piece of legerdemain, Hall addressed this problem by giving his *Henrys* a Brechtian impression. The hand-wrought effect of John Bury's scenery belonged to this motive, as did an abundance of real objects that filled the stage for the actors to use – things that looked hard and uncomfortable, built for utility and handled over a long time. The King's bedroom had wooden furniture, unpainted, hand-hewn, and styled only for the 90-degree angle. No one but the sick or the exhausted would use it, but the King, as played by Eric Porter, was sick and exhausted. A crucifix hung on one of the riveted walls, with a rugged altar beneath it for kneeling. The King was attended by monk-like physicians clothed in black. One of them ground some ingredients in a mortar – the King's medicine was being prepared, and the harshness of such stuff could almost be tasted by the audience.

In the second scene (usually said to occur in 'a room in the Prince's house'), Falstaff and Hal made their entrance in a haycart, bumping along on large wooden wheels and pulled by Bardolph and Peto. They woke up by dousing themselves at a real water pump. Later, the tavern scenes were filled with detail. A fire burned in a brazier, where Hal, a little disgusted by what he had just read, burned Falstaff's tavern reckoning. Mistress Quickly had shirts to dry and a bed to make. The tavern was busy with patrons. It was a place where real work had to be done. Such concentration on the people and objects of common life was part of an overall Brechtian influence on the production, although one wondered if even the Berliner Ensemble would go to the length of having real donkeys for Bardolph and Falstaff to ride as they journeyed to Coventry in Act IV.

The Brechtian influence had run strong in London since 1956, when the Berliner Ensemble made their first visit, performing *Mother Courage*, *Drums and Trumpets*, and *The Caucasian Chalk Circle* at the Palace Theatre. A group of talented young directors, designers, and performers, most of them just down from university (a number of them just down from Cambridge), was moving into the London theatre at the same time: they included Hall, Barton,

Bury, and Clifford Williams, just to name the directors and the designer of the RSC Shakespeare cycle to come. Many important events occurred in the London theatre at about this time – the first production of *Waiting for Godot*, which Hall himself directed, for example, and the formation of the English Stage Company to produce new plays at the Royal Court – and among the various innovations and influences that shaped the Royal Shakespeare Company of the 1960s, the Berliner Ensemble must be ranked high.

The Berliner stood for an ensemble style developed through the stability of a long-term subsidised company, an artistic conviction that the stage should show the real objects and structures of social experience rather than the trappings of a single ruling class, and a political determination to emphasise the values and humanity of common people in the interests of socialism. Of those elements the English learned all but the political. To build an ensemble over the years, to gain a subsidy for it, to construct its staging around the objects and structures of everyday use – these artistic lessons were carried fully into the Royal Shakespeare Company. For a time even the political emphasis seemed to take hold. The company was thought to be 'radical' because it took on controversial modern plays and because many of its productions, certainly including the history cycle, demonstrated the brutality of power held remote from the people. The promise of such a beginning did not carry into a coherent politics, however, and the Royal Shakespeare Company, as its name would indicate, was really taking root in ruling-class soil in order to put forth occasional left-wing blossoms.

As for the particular Brechtian emphasis of *1 Henry IV*, one can see with the benefit of hindsight that Hall was being inconsistent. His idea of a 'just proportion in all things' working through the machinery of power politics is antithetical to Brechtian theory and practice. But few noticed this at the time. What passed for left-wing cultural politics in 1964 was a cheerful and broad-minded business, encompassing the Beatles and the mini-skirt along with the Royal Shakespeare Company. For Hall to introduce lessons from the Berliner Ensemble into his thinking about order and the power machine without being caught out and charged with contradiction required genial and muddled thinking all round. Hall was not caught out. Everyone noticed that the Brechtian emphasis of the 1964 plays did not match up to the design of the previous year's *Wars of the Roses*, but this was a minor stylistic issue for most. After

[59]

all, Brecht was fashionable.

One critic did explicitly challenge the borrowing from Brecht. His complaint was not that Hall was contradicting himself, but that he was not living up to Shakespeare's intentions. The critic was Ronald Bryden of *The New Statesman*, and his complaint was part of a larger challenge to the idea of the cycle in the first place. The plays were not written as part of a unified scheme, Bryden argued, especially not a unified scheme that portrayed the education of Prince Hal. Shakespeare 'made no attempt to explain the changes by which ... the wild Prince Hal turned into a chivalrous monarch. The transformations are part of the myth' (*New Statesman*, 24 April 1964). The plays are different sorts of pieces – *Richard III* is a Machiavellian tragedy, *Richard II* 'an ornately Spenserian hagiography'. The real object of criticism, however, was the directorial team of Hall, Barton, and Williams. 'The plays have been totally and masterfully produced, and they have been produced wrong', Bryden announced, and he went on to complain of the Brechtian quality of the staging. As the wagons were pulled into muddy farmyards, 'I looked for Mother Courage to follow with her children.'

The potentially interesting challenge to Hall – that resorting to Brecht was a contradiction to his own conception of the cycle – here gets caught up in the appeal everyone was making in 1964, the appeal to Shakespeare's intentions. The Quadricentennial celebration encouraged even more talk than is usual about what Shakespeare intended. It was now the standard opinion that Shakespeare's histories were planned as a cycle, and that the newly subsidised Royal Shakespeare Company should be cherished for recovering those intentions by staging the whole thing. Bryden was standing out from the crowd by challenging this point (and not standing out from the crowd forever, as we shall see in the next chapter). His review was notable because it reversed the usual approach and declared what Shakespeare did *not* intend, namely a cycle. (There is no way to know that either, of course, but if Shakespearians could consistently talk about what their author did not intend, he would eventually be declared to have intended nothing, and the field would be clear of the question of intention.) The other reviewers, finding it more convenient to take the positive approach to the intentions, applauded the scale and intention of the huge RSC undertaking. 'I doubt if anything as valuable has ever been done for Shakespeare in the whole previous history of the world's stage', said Harold Hobson when *1 Henry IV* opened and linked up with the rest of the cycle (*Sunday Times*, 19 April 1964), and such hyperbole seemed convincing in those heady days.

* * *

On the individual performances in *1 Henry IV*, some doubts were mixed in with the praise. Hugh Griffith's Falstaff drew the widest extremes of response. Griffith had come in from the outside. He did not take part in the *Wars of the Roses* plays of 1963 and he was one of the few actors who was not doubling roles across the cycle. Falstaff does come from nowhere, in a sense, so the decision to cast him from outside the earlier plays had some justification, and Griffith was a veteran Rabelaisian performer, recently acclaimed for his Squire Western in the film of *Tom Jones*. He seemed a natural choice, and many reviewers liked his performance. His Falstaff was 'a gigantic eye-rolling, grey-bearded Mephistopheles' (*Evening Standard*, 17 April 1964). Set within his gross bulk was 'a sharp mobile face capable of quicksilver changes between craftiness, mock-gravity, and tenderness' (*The Times*, 17 April 1964). One can hear recollections of Richardson's Falstaff in those descriptions – the quick eye, the sharp voice – but another influence was Quayle's 1951 performance (Griffith had played Glendower in that production). Quayle had hardened the character, delivering a rogue more dangerous than jolly, and Griffith was adept at working the same vein. He was putting Richardson's swift eye and mind together with Quayle's edge of menace: 'And then his eyes – how they roved! How they rolled! How they flashed – beacons of anarchy in an England which was trying to reduce itself to order!' (Robert Speaight, 'Shakespeare in Britain,' p. 383).

At the centre of these image-shattering productions, then, was a Falstaff of traditional alignments, reminding one of the good Falstaffs of 1945 and 1951. That is the wrong way around, when one stops to think about it – Falstaff is supposed to be the unorthodox one. Perhaps that is why some critics noticed that Griffith was a bit off the beat: he caught the role 'fitfully' (*The Birmingham Post*, 17 April 1964); he had a 'yet imperfect hold on the lines' (*Daily Mail* 17 April 1964). What the rest of the company had learned about power-politics and iconoclasm through a year of performing the earlier histories had to be learned by Hugh Griffith in a month of rehearsals, and the sense that this *1 Henry IV* was not quite right, not quite in keeping with the accomplishment of the earlier plays, came to some extent from a Falstaff who would have been more at home in another production of the play.

But there may be no way to do with Falstaff what this production was doing with the other characters – turn them a bit towards parody, give them an edge of exaggeration. How does one exaggerate Falstaff? Roy Dotrice showed how one can exaggerate Hotspur. You take a famous earlier performance and push its mannerisms a little harder. Dotrice took Redgrave's Hotspur, with its research into Northern dialect and horsemanship, and worked it into 'a mad music-hall Macduff in kilt and flaming red hair' (*Observer*, 19 April 1964). Redgrave's burred 'R' Dotrice turned to a Scots accent just as flamboyant as his kilt and flaming red hair. His scenes with Lady Percy (Janet Suzman) carried the boisterousness of Redgrave and Barbara Jefford to the point of rolling on the floor, sitting on one another, and having a great romp of an undignified time. His 'If I mistake not, thou art Harry Monmouth' at the beginning of the single combat at Shrewsbury (V. iv. 57) was accompanied by a chortle as he went flying at Hal with a huge two-handed sword raised over his head. There was unquestionably an element of cartoon in this performance, which vividly projected the kind of rebel Hal would have to reject on his way to the crown. But to show Falstaff in the same light of exaggeration may well have been impossible. He is already there.

Hal was played by Ian Holm, a relatively unknown actor who had the enormous assignments of turning the Prince into Henry V in the first half of the cycle and Gloucester into Richard III in the second. This Hal troubled the critics, who respected Holm's diligence, his sense of timing, and his intelligence, without much liking his performance. His Hal was unpredictable, given to bouts of withdrawn and uncongenial behaviour just when he seemed ready to enjoy himself among his Eastcheap cronies. This led onlookers to suppose he was playing Burton's kind of Hal, giving a realistic psychological portrayal of a cold-blooded young man who was working his way towards heroism. Yet some reviewers sensed that something quite different from psychological realism and consistency was being offered in Holm's performance. He may have been one member of the company who was actually carrying the Brechtian motive of the cycle to its logical end, to the point of breaking with the interests of psychological realism and becoming a commentator on the character he was demonstrating. Those who found him too 'detached' for Hal may have been exactly right, although they tended to dislike the quality they were right about.

One of Holm's critics was Gareth Lloyd Evans, whose account of Holm's weaknesses gains an extra dimension if read in the light of Brecht's ideas about acting:

> His main weakness is to impersonate rather than interpret … . He tends, that is, to act from the outside of a character, and to engage in tricksiness of speech and gesture. Diligent preparation for a role … does not seem to compensate, in him, for an occasional demonstration of a playfulness of spirit. This never lets him down in a strictly theatrical sense, but prevents him from a final engagement with the character. ('The Twentieth Century and "Behaviourism"', p. 137: this review is based on Holm's performance in a revival of the Stratford production in 1966, but I believe it reflects his performance in 1964 as well.)

In the first tavern scene, to give a detailed example of the effect of Holm's detached reading, when Falstaff went off to answer the door, Hal's exchange with Bardolph and the others was not the comic indictment of the old rogue that it usually is. Instead, Hal stared the others down and startled them with little bursts of ironic laughter (Wharton, p. 68), until they pressed around him eager to side with him against Falstaff – a demonstration not of tavern camaraderie but of a figure of authority manipulating a crowd. This was a preview of *Henry V*, where the Hal of the Boar's Head would become the hero of Agincourt manipulating his soldiers. In a sense, Henry V was already on hand as Hal controlled the tavern group.

In the play-acting that followed, Falstaff offered what Hal ought to have sought according to a psychological reading, a little fatherly contact. Hal's own father, the Henry IV of Eric Porter, was remote and unapproachable, but Falstaff showed warm feeling and caressed Hal's face while acting the father's role. Holm did not spurn such gestures. It was clear that he appreciated them, but equally clear that they would not displace his condemnation of the disreputable old man. When it came time for the response to Falstaff's 'banish plump Jack and banish all the world', Holm was waiting for him, his reply already thought out. 'I do', then a long pause as he looked into the old man's face, then a pitiless 'I will.'

Griffith gave a determined roar of laughter to that, but it was as though his rejection had already taken place, and there was no avoiding its implications. Holm's Prince was built with one dimension in our time, as though he could look back and see himself. This accomplishment Gareth Lloyd Evans, still in a critical vein, caught perfectly in his description of the earlier 'I know you all' soliloquy:

Holm 'gives the impression of being an onlooker, not from another area of society, but from another time (ours)' ('Twentieth Century and "Behaviourism"', p. 137). In a more admiring vein, Alan Dent said of the 'I do, I will' exchange, 'Time seems suddenly to transpose us all across the centuries, so that the past, for as much as a whole minute or two, seems much more real than the present' (*The Financial Times*, 17 April 1964). That is not exactly what Brecht had in mind (nor is *The Financial Times*). We are not supposed to be 'transposed' into the past in this kind of performance but given a perspective on the past from a position clearly established in the present. That Holm was doing that for one critic who complained while another was happily being transposed into the past suggests at least a complex performance.

The staging of the Battle of Shrewsbury scenes shows how these elements came together. One might recall the picturesque arrangement in the Old Vic production of 1945, when Olivier's Hotspur delivered his final speech standing and clutching his death wound, then crashed down two steps on to his face to struggle with his final stammered 'w', all this taking place before a vista showing fields and a distant cathedral. In 1964 there was no vista. Instead, the stage was closed in by John Bury's massive walls, which parted far enough to show an impenetrable thicket just behind. Near the thicket was a pig trough – this was a Shrewsbury farmyard. In this closed-in space, with no hint of Merrie England in the background, the battles were frightening. Douglas came at the King with a real mace. The King was so enfeebled that he had no chance on his own, although he was wily enough to get over to the pig trough and gain time by throwing swill at his assailant. Hal saved his father by dint of fierce attacks with sword and dagger. Holm is small of build, but both as Hal and as Richard III (where he used ball and chain) he could outfight bigger men by knowing his weapons and moving quickly.

Dotrice's Hotspur was one of those bigger men, and when he launched himself at Hal with his delighted chortle – one reviewer said he was 'moved by war to sensual ecstasy' (*The Times*, 17 April 1964) – it looked as though size would win out. On and on they fought, Hotspur swinging a huge two-handed broadsword against Hal's sword and dagger. The broadsword looked as if it could cut right through a smaller man. One feared injuries not to Hal but to Ian Holm. John Barton's expertise with stage fights was taking hold. There seemed to be no way for Hal to win this battle – but we were not reckoning on the pig trough. Hotspur missed with a swipe of the broadsword; it slammed into the side of the trough and seemed to stick there for a second. Hal had time to slip his dagger in under Hotspur's armour and tip him into the swill. Anti-heroism can do no more with the Battle of Shrewsbury than dump Hotspur into a pig trough. It was a tremendously menacing and disturbing fight, a demonstration of the battlefield brutality that ran through the entire cycle, and one took no pleasure in knowing that a hero-King of England was emerging out of such violence.

* * *

It is best to draw back from this particular stage-moment and recall the circumstances in which it occurred. *1 Henry IV* opened in April 1964 as part of Stratford's celebration of Shakespeare's 400th birthday. The Duke of Edinburgh was there; so were the President of the World Bank and the representatives of over 100 nations, whose flags were dramatically unfurled along the streets of Stratford in a time-honoured birthday celebration. In all, 750 members of the diplomatic corps were there. Everyone was pleased to learn that £200,000 had been raised for the new Shakespeare Centre in Stratford, out of a £500,000 goal. On the stairway of the Centre was a carpet given by the Shah of Persia (*Yorkshire Post*, 17 April 1964).

The RSC has never had so many influential productions in hand as those being staged or planned in that April. The full cycle of the Shakespeare histories was being completed. The Aldwych season in London, about to be announced, would begin with revivals of three major contemporary plays: Pinter's *Birthday Party*, David Rudkin's *'Afore Night Come*, and Beckett's *Endgame*. These would all be opened by 9 July, after which would come the British première of Tirso de Molina's *Green Stockings*, to be followed by another première in August, the *Marat/Sade* of Peter Weiss, in a production by Peter Brook that would have enormous impact for generations to come. To attain such a balance of success between Stratford and London was itself a great achievement, but the RSC also had the Brook–Paul Scofield *King Lear* on world tour, together with Clifford Williams' wonderful production of *Comedy of Errors*. Both of *those* productions would also influence future Shakespearian performance. It would be hard to name a more significant period for one company's importance in the theatre at large than this period of mid-1964 for the Royal Shakespeare Company.

For many of its followers, the company had a progressive politi-

[65]

cal reputation. For a time in England in the 1960s it seemed as if theatre could change the world. Some of the people who shared that belief were with the RSC, and many were in their audiences. The company's success was charged with an energy that could easily be converted into left-wing political claims. The contradiction between socialist politics and an institution that was 'royal' by name, patronised by the well-to-do, and unattended by the working class was not yet making itself felt. It was possible for Peter Hall to speak of a popular revolution in the theatre, even as the Shah's rug was being installed at the Shakespeare Centre and the Duke of Edinburgh was preparing to attend the theatre where Hotspur would be dumped in the pig trough. 'Given low enough seat prices,' Hall said, 'the theatre could undergo a popular revolution. The masses who buy paperbacks would stream into it' (quoted in the *Birmingham Mail*, 16 April 1964).

This kind of talk was perfectly sincere and perfectly unrealistic. Hall's real interest in 1964 lay in obtaining a new London theatre for the company, for the Aldwych was not a profitable venture despite the importance of the plays staged there. The new theatre would remain the company's urgent need for nearly two decades, a period during which Hall would leave the RSC, complete a term as Director of the National Theatre, and look ahead to founding his own commercial company devoted to staging the classics at West End prices.

By the time the RSC's new London theatre opened at the Barbican in 1982, the company would have staged a new *1 Henry IV* as part of a cycle for the 1970s and would be readying another *1 Henry IV* as part of the cycle for the early 1980s (the late 1980s would see a cycle of the *early* history plays). The first of these productions will be the subject of the next chapter, but here we are glancing ahead from Hall's comment about a popular revolution in the theatre to see if the revolutionary spirit would take hold in the later history of the RSC, and we are finding a magnificent new theatre, a 'jewel set in a concrete sea', as Peter Hall's successor as artistic director termed the Barbican, but what we are not finding is cheap seats for the masses. Earlier I mentioned that one could attend the Richardson–Olivier Old Vic production for the price of ten to forty cigarettes. Had one purchased anything for the price of ten to forty cigarettes at the Barbican in 1982 it would have been either cigarettes or a sausage roll in the Waterside Café. The high ticket prices would be blamed on inflation and inadequate government subsidies (the RSC subsidy has always been lower than the National Theatre's), but the underlying question is whether the new theatre at the Barbican, with its aura of middle-class grandeur and its extreme operating expenses, was not bound to define the RSC once and for all as the creature of corporate and government interests. It had been RSC policy in the days of apparent political progressivism *not* to offer advantages for those who gave extra money, for example, but patrons' subscription benefits were established in 1980 when the costs of the Barbican became apparent (Beauman, *Royal Shakespeare Company*, p. 349). By 1990 there were four levels of 'corporate membership,' ranging from £1,800 to £11,000 annually, with such advantages as 'best seats for RSC productions, social and entertainment facilities, priority booking and advanced information privileges, and prestigious publicity' (1990 theatre programme for *All's Well That Ends Well*, price £1-50).

The artistic policy of the company during these twenty-five years of expansion and rising prices has been steered away from politics and toward the representation of psychological essences in the human character, primarily in the male human character. That, at any rate, is what one finds in tracing the company's involvement with Shakespeare's history plays, an interpretation that will be documented in the next chapter. For the moment, I wish to note how early the change occurred, at least in the pronouncements of Peter Hall. As early as May 1964, while the full range of the history cycle was still new and those important plays mentioned above were touring or being planned, Hall announced that the socially-committed theatre 'has spent its force now' (*Plays and Players*, May, 1964). The new plays being written are 'about ritual murder or the lusts of Man and all that'. What 'all that' amounted to, besides Man's lust and ritual murder, Hall did not say, but he thought Shakespeare was actually writing about it: 'we're beginning to understand that the thing underlying Shakespeare's plays, far more than the political, moral, and ethical things of the Elizabethan era, is an awareness of the Theatre of Ritual and of Man's basic passions'. Try to govern Man's basic passions and you are in for hard work. They are 'recurring patterns of human behaviour which come from instinct, and this is almost ungovernable'. Amidst these almost ungovernable instincts, it seems clear there is nothing for politics to do.

One admires the honesty of such commentary. Unlike remarks about a revolution in the theatre, it implies the company's real ties and its real standing in the theatre world. Power will always find it advantageous for cultural institutions to show human nature as unchanging and yet theatrical. That it is theatrical makes it stageworthy, that it is unchanging makes it, in the long run, safe. I say 'in the long run' because Hall's 1964 remarks about the recurring patterns of human behaviour looked ahead to the Theatre of Cruelty experiments and the *Marat/Sade* production, ventures which were anything but tame. With Peter Brook directing and with Artaud's theories being summoned from the past to give intellectual backing, it was hard to fret about the implications for political theatre, and many thought Brook's productions were political anyhow. The 'long run' lasted beyond the 1960s and the departures of Brook and Hall from the company. By the mid-1970s the change had occurred. Left-wing politics and Artaud must still have played some part in a company so varied and energetic as the RSC, but financial difficulties were now the problem that had to be remedied. The history plays were called upon, once again in a cycle format, but this time the venture was kept free of the apparent political progressivism of the 1960s.

CHAPTER V

1975. The Royal Shakespeare Company: Terry Hands

In 1975 the Royal Shakespeare Company mounted another cycle of the *Henrys*, this time opening with the last in Shakespeare's series, *Henry V*, and adding the *Henry IV* plays shortly thereafter, then the other Falstaff play, *The Merry Wives of Windsor*. The director of the entire series was Terry Hands, who took care to set his version of the history plays apart from the 1964 cycle by stressing that this time the plays would not be primarily political. '*The Wars of the Roses* was a study in power politics,' Hands later wrote, alluding to the 1964 cycle. 'Its central image was the conference table. ... But that's not Shakespeare. Shakespeare goes far beyond politics. Politics is a very shallow science' (Trussler, 1980/81, pp. 54-5). What took the place of the shallow science of politics, Hands went on, was kingship: 'Kings have been out of fashion for a long time. People are embarrassed by them. But our leaders still have almost divine power.' Exactly how an interest in kingship can be separated from an interest in politics was not spelled out in these remarks, but the greatest interest of Hands' production of *1 Henry IV* lay in the nerve-racking relationship between father and son portrayed by Emrys James as Henry IV and Alan Howard as Prince Hal, together with a staging and blocking design that emphasised the inner theatricality of the play, and such matters of domestic relationship and the theatre can seem non-political when they are raised to a high pitch of excitement.

In an earlier comment, Hands did specify his reasons for beginning the season with *Henry V* (Beauman, *Henry IV*, pp. 15-16). He

[69]

wanted the opening Chorus of that play to be the keynote of the season, which was going to present a stripped-down, back-to-basics Royal Shakespeare Company. On a stage bare of scenery and extra properties, a smaller company than usual – twenty-five, compared to nearly twice that number in the 1964 cycle – would be 'the flat unraised spirits that have dared / On this unworthy scaffold to bring forth / So great an object' as *Henry V* (Prologue, 9-11). Or at least they would begin that way. They would begin in rehearsal clothes, gradually take on historical costumes, and finally coalesce into a unified company upon the King's 'Saint Crispin's Day' speech at Agincourt. Thus the 'band of brothers' would be twice-born: they would be the soldiers on the field of Agincourt, they would be the company on the stage of the Shakespeare Memorial Theatre.

The reason for stripping down the company and beginning with a rehearsal device was, as everyone freely admitted, financial. The Royal Shakespeare Company was itself being stripped down. In part the problem had arisen from the most successful aspect of the Peter Hall regime: opening a London base at the Aldwych Theatre in the 1960s certainly extended the company's range and influence, but the Aldwych always ran a deficit. Now, with the annual deficit mounting, came a new financial hardship. Inflation raged through capitalist societies between 1973 and 1975, largely as a result of the Arab oil embargo. Production costs rose sharply, and the deficit worsened. In March, before the 1975 season began, the RSC Artistic Director, Trevor Nunn, published the bad news. The company was cutting back its repertory by one-third, was abandoning its season at the Aldwych in London, and was ending its small-theatre experimental work (*Guardian*, 8 March 1975).

So with minimalism the order of the day, the RSC staged their non-political histories, and the season turned out to be a financial success. Thanks in part to a special Centenary Appeal for funds and a last-minute infusion of extra money from the Arts Council, a massive deficit was turned into a small surplus by early 1976. The 1975 *Henry V* was one of the company's most successful productions ever, both in critical and financial terms. The RSC even had a book written about it (Beauman, *Henry IV*). The preface to that book, signed simply 'Philip' and stamped with the royal seal, showed how distant were the days when Peter Hall mused about attracting a working-class audience to the theatre. 'Philip' in his preface was adding another group to the 'band of brothers' who fought so bravely at Agincourt. These were the 'band of supporters' of the RSC, who faced the 'menace of rising costs and inflation' in the same spirit as Henry's 'tiny, hungry, ill clad band of troops under its hero King facing a huge, well armed and confident army'. The 1960s were certainly over now. And the RSC was setting about redefining itself through some of the same history plays that had shaped Peter Hall's troupe a decade before.

* * *

If the proper starting-point for a season of austerity is the opening of *Henry V*, where does that place the *Henry IV* plays? How does one perform something that comes before the beginning? This was a dilemma which the 1975 company never finally solved, and I shall discuss this difficulty at the end of the present chapter. The battle to break out of the impasse, however, produced some flashes of innovation which deserve to be seen first. Hands rehearsed *1 Henry IV* and *Henry V* together, working on each play for half the day, and a great deal of thought was obviously given to the relationships between the plays. If *Henry V* was to be the occasion for establishing a renewed acting company, for example, it became possible to search both it and *1 Henry IV* for signs of self-conscious theatricality – perhaps a concern for acting in the formation of a royal personality, for example. When the royal personality being formed is that of Prince Hal / Henry V, one does not have to search far for the theatre. Hal's first scene ends with a soliloquy announcing that his Eastcheap licentiousness is a deliberate piece of acting, a prelude to his deliberate transformation from scapegrace to royal hero. In the first tavern scene, he plays Falstaff to Falstaff's Henry IV, then switches places and enacts the King in a prefiguration of his eventual role. Every production since Richard Burton's in 1951 had emphasised the psychological seriousness of this moment. When Hal says he will banish Falstaff – 'I do, I will' – the modern theatre has come to understand that he is 'rehearsing' an event which he will have to 'perform' as King, and this recognition can be turned outward to the play as a whole and carried further in *Henry V*, where, on the night before the Battle of Agincourt, the King is acting the role of a common soldier. Hal / Henry V literally plays more roles than any other character in Shakespeare, and when he is not busy talking about the nature of the theatre in such moments as the 'I know you all' soliloquy in *1 Henry IV* or his meditation on 'ceremony' in *Henry V*, he is very likely to be hearing his father's voice saying he is not enough of an actor, not half as good as *I* was.

There must have been exhilarating moments as rehearsals moved back and forth between *Henry V* and *1 Henry IV*, moments when it seemed that the centre of Shakespeare's later histories had been found in this correspondence between the text's attention to theatricality and the company's attention to its own theatrical reformation. The designer, Abdel Farrah, had the proscenium of the Stratford theatre stripped to bare brick and the back wall uncovered. He wanted the stage to be visible as just that, a stage, and the audience to see it as part of the building they were sitting in. He then tilted the acting space towards the auditorium by means of a steeply raked stage floor, one in twelve. 'It was a stage designed to launch the actors into the audience,' he said. 'The comment that pleased me most was that it was like the great deck of an aircraft carrier. It meant that the actors on the stage were very clearly defined, and that they too were metaphorically stripped.... It wasn't a stage where you could hide weakness' (quoted in Beauman, *Henry IV*, p. 31). The wayward simile in that comment – if the stage is to resemble a stage, why should it be good to hear that it resembled an aircraft carrier? – can be allowed to pass in favour of the excitement that drives the statement, for this, it can be imagined, is a version of the excitement driving the entire performance. A company that many thought on the verge of failure was turning their very peril into the discovery of Shakespearian meanings, and that is the combination – success contrived on the risk of failure – that generates all moments of theatrical excitement, large and small.

Farrah allowed himself one spectacular device – a great canopy that would unfurl over the action to form a beautiful roof for the major scenes. 'It looked baroque, and yet it also looked Asiatic', Farrah said, and he took pleasure in contriving these impressions out of the material used for circus tents, cotton duck. The canopy was used for all of the history plays in 1975, giving scenic unity to the narrative sweep and diversity of the plays, as Tanya Moiseiwitsch had done with her timber-frame structure in 1951. As in 1951, some confusion hung over this conception: just as some had wondered why Moiseiwitsch's royal court looked so like the Boar's Head, their descendants now wondered why the entrance to the tavern should look like a tent. Realism never loses its hold over some imaginations. Yet the canopy was widely appreciated for its spectacular beauty, not to mention its small cost, and it permitted a brilliant effect in the battle scenes. The colourful emblazoned roof would descend to settle on to the stage floor and, revealing its other side, plain brown, would become the muddy field of Shrewsbury or Agincourt. Thus the battle scenes had soldiers trampling over the cloth that otherwise formed the ceremonial displays of their nations.

When duck cloth can be made to do all that, penury has been turned into invention. The design of this production was constantly drawing fresh insight out of its minimalist necessities. Suppose there is not a great deal of money to furnish each scene with its own properties. Why not leave the properties of one scene in place to serve for the next? But what if those scenes are drastically different locations – the Boar's Head tavern, then Glendower's castle in Wales, then the royal court in London, then the Boar's Head again? All the better, replies the minimalist. Run them together with the same properties and provoke the audiences to some hard thinking. Why should Falstaff in the tavern sit in the same chair that the King has just been sitting in at Court? Does that insist on some similarity between the two? The 1951 single set had led to such doubling in the uses of the furniture, but Hands carried the idea further and applied it to stage properties as well. The map that Glendower, Mortimer, and Hotspur used to divide the kingdom in their Welsh scene was left lying on the stage for the King to point at in the next scene when he forced his son into some sense of royal responsibility. He did not see what we knew the map contained. It was already marked with the rebel's division of the kingdom. In the same scene, Hal reacted to his father's pressure by crossing to a barrel from the tavern scene and seizing a pint-pot of sack left there – a sign that his Eastcheap waywardness was a defence against the overbearing King. By the end of the scene, as a sort of forced reconciliation was reached between them, the father was taking a swig from the same pot.

In all of Shakespeare it would be hard to find four consecutive scenes so varied and yet so sustained along a major narrative line as the four from which the above examples are chosen: the first tavern scene (with the discomfiting of Falstaff and the play-acting between Falstaff and Hal), the Glendower scene (with its argument among the rebels and its lyrical closing in the Welsh song of Lady Mortimer), the first of the 'rebuke' scenes between father and son at Court, and the second tavern scene (which concludes with preparations for war and Falstaff's demand for breakfast). The modern theatre nearly always breaks this succession with an interval after the first tavern scene, but Hands held the scenes together by placing

[73]

one interval early, before the first tavern scene, and another later, after the second tavern scene. This allowed him to 'overlap' the four scenes I have mentioned, which now formed the middle stretch of action. In addition to using the same properties for the different locations, Hands often had his actors overlap too, with those from the scene just concluded staying on to watch the beginning of the new scene, or those from the new scene arriving early to watch the preceding one; and this blending of scenes worked together with the overlap of properties to give the impression of a flow of observed action rather than an assembly of discrete units.

Although the overlapping of scenes seemed especially pronounced in the middle stretch of action, it occurred elsewhere as well. At the end of the opening scene, for example, the King and his courtiers moved to the back of the stage and stayed for a few minutes to observe Hal and Falstaff in the early part of I. ii. At the conclusion of I. ii, Hal finished his 'I know you all' soliloquy, crossed to stage right, and moved upstage, while the King and the rebellious lords entered and began the next scene. 'Watches Court' is how the prompt book describes Hal at this point, and this is the repeated cue for the overlapping actors. They are always 'watching' part of the new scene.

Such blending of scenes annoyed some reviewers. Richard David gave the most substantial criticism when he said that running the locations together, which some had thought an 'Elizabethan' technique, actually ran athwart the coherence of the placeless Elizabethan stage. The Elizabethan stage never came to stand for any of a play's fictional locations, David noted. It always retained its own identity as a stage, just the impression Farrah was seeking when he was not hearing about aircraft carriers, and its connection with the fictional locations was imaginatively fluid. But 'the curious tied-notes between scenes' in Hands' production, David said, 'so far from proving that the stage is at the same time everywhere and nowhere, call attention to its precise localisations and so sacrifice the peculiar Elizabethan advantage' (David, 1978, p. 195).

That assumes, of course, that Hands was trying for the effect of Elizabethan staging. No one from the production said anything about that. They more readily said they were trying to cut costs in order to solve a problem imposed by an Arts Council whose subsidy was not keeping pace with inflation. As an artistic motive, the tying-together of locations through unchanging properties seems instead to be connected with the device of having characters from one scene observe those enacting another. If the Boar's Head was the same space as Court, the observer from the tavern scene merely lingers and watches the King at Court. But why should the characters watch one another? The answer was not apparent to the early reviewers. One thought a sort of Special Branch or CIA twist was being given to these spied-upon affairs of the fifteenth century, adding that this was unnecessary: 'there is enough in the text to demonstrate how speedily the adversaries' intelligence service worked' (*The Times*, 25 April 1975). Another thought the father and son watched one another as a sign of the bond that unites them, 'so that the one is always on the other's mind' (David, 1978, p. 194).

Neither *Mission Impossible* or *Father Knows Best* was at work here, though. A glance at the programme would have given the whole thing away. This was larded with quotations from Erving Goffman, Eric Berne, and B. F. Skinner (and St Augustine, Hamlet, Sartre, Beckett, Oliver Goldsmith, T. S. Eliot – this was a time-consuming programme) about the psychology of role-playing in everyday life. 'A part once played honestly and in earnest leaves the performer in a position to contrive a showing of it later' (Goffman). 'When I was not obeyed, because people did not understand me, I was angry and I avenged myself on them by tears' (St Augustine). 'When someone behaves in a way we find laudable we make him more likely to do so again by praising or commending him' (Skinner). 'Let us consider this waiter in the café. His movement is quick and forward, a little too rapid. He comes towards the patrons with a step a little too quick. He bends forward a little too eagerly... . He is playing at being a waiter in a café' (Sartre). As I have noted, the theatre was being made especially conscious of itself in Hands' interpretation of the plays, and the device of 'watching' was part of this motif. The actors / characters were watching one another stage their scenes so that the role-playing being done within the play as written would have a layer of spectatorship just beyond the text, there on the edge of the stage, where actors not involved in a scene would be learning how scenes can be done. The learning is also being done by the characters, of course. That was Henry IV watching how his son behaves at the Boar's Head, as well as Emrys James watching Alan Howard. The idea works for actor and character at once.

If it works at all, that is. Some of the 'watching' manoeuvres were merely awkward and had to be changed. Originally, as Richard David saw the Glendower scene, 'a muffled figure appeared high in a sort of belfry in Glendower's hall. One expected it to turn into the fairy harpist summoned by Glendower; but no, it was Henry IV, who as the Welsh party broke up came awkwardly down a ladder to receive his truant son.' This bit of watching was obviously not working, so it was modified into the version now preserved in the prompt-book. During Lady Mortimer's song, the King entered downstage left and Hal entered downstage right, to observe the end of the Glendower scene. As the Glendower actors exited, the courtiers called for at the beginning of the next scene, the royal interview, moved into position at the rear of the stage. The King's lines dismissing the courtiers were cut, however, and there they stayed throughout the entire father–son colloquy, a row of observers dimly seen at the rear, suggesting that privacy is hard to attain at this theatrical Court. (In 1964, with Ian Holm playing Hal, Holm was so concerned to have privacy that he went over and closed the door before replying to his father's 'how much thou art degenerate' – III. ii. 128.)

Thus the King and Prince began the scene by addressing one another over a vast distance from opposite sides of the stage, with the courtiers visible upstage centre. At the King's 'God pardon thee' (l. 29), they moved towards the centre of the stage, with Hal keeping his distance by crossing to the barrel left on from the tavern scene – a bit of Eastcheap protection during the rebuke that followed. The prompt-book charmingly announces at this point: 'From here on anything can happen.' (Ian Judge, Assistant Director of the 1975 production, told me this was an acknowledgement of Emrys James's tendency to vary the staging each time.) What the prompt-book calls for is a sort of wrestling of Hal into forced unity with his father. At Hal's vow to redeem himself at Hotspur's expense: 'King stands, goes to hug Hal. Stops. Looks away. Holds out hand. Hal takes it. King H. pulls Hal onto chair. Embrace.' Then Blunt comes down from the group of courtiers: 'Hal sees him & stops embrace.' After Blunt's speech, 'Hal escapes from King H., crosses to barrel – pick up glass.'

The psychological struggle of this father–son relationship seems clearly marked out by the intended blocking, especially by Hal's use of the tavern-scene properties as a defence against the overbearing demands of the King. The 'watching' motif intrudes upon privacy, reminding one that role-playing and theatricality require public displays at the expense of intimacy. I see nothing particularly Elizabethan about any of this. The intentions seem decidedly modern, yet in line with implications in the text. This royal father and son are certainly involved in psychological tension of some sort, and if the actors give a particularly physical, 'anything can happen' interpretation to this possibility, they are not violating the general implication of the scene so much as they are demonstrating one of its more extreme possibilities. As I have discussed in Chapter II, on the 1951 production, the concern for theatricality in this father–son colloquy is not just an implication. The King blames Hal explicitly for not knowing how to handle the staging of his own role, quite overlooking his son's originality on exactly this point (III. ii. 39-80). Hands' interpretation was meeting the text on its own terms and giving it a clear modern extension. Conceptually, this was as interesting and innovative a version of the father–son relationship as the modern theatre is likely to afford.

* * *

Strong conceptions can be carried too far. A number of reviewers thought that the point of no return was reached in the performance of Emrys James as Henry IV. I have mentioned the prompt-book's admission that efforts to record the blocking of an Emrys James scene will fail to capture the variety of the actual event. James was a rigorously independent, thoughtful actor, and his reading of the royal personality of Henry IV broke the patience of some observers. Prince Hal was supposed to be the neurotic, after Richard Burton's performance set the standard for that role in 1951, and anyone familiar with Alan Howard's career in the theatre will know that *his* Hal had a knife-edge of anxiety about it. But the King was supposed to be more stable. He had been strong and worried in 1951 (Harry Andrews), fretful and ill in 1964 (Eric Porter), distant and melodious in the Welles film of 1966 (John Gielgud) – but no one before Emrys James played him as 'a father any son would be glad to escape, … a snarling, sardonic, guilt-laden autocrat' (*The Times*, 25 April 1975), or 'piggy-eyed' and 'able to persuade himself only by violence of speech and action' (*Financial Times*, 25 April 1975). This was 'an inexplicable mistake in casting', said one critic. 'Neither the mailed fist nor the arts of popular appeal which had brought [the King] to the throne were apparent in an hysterical exercise of authority' (Speaight, 'Shakespeare in Britain', p. 18).

Yet James's performance was riveting, and many of the details the reviewers recalled were etched by him. In his early scene with the northern rebels, he burst out with a high scream on the thought of revolted Mortimer ('No, on the barren mountains let him starve' – I. iii. 89), then actually threw down a coin on the following line about not giving 'one penny' in ransom. Hotspur – especially hot-headed in Stuart Wilson's interpretation – moved towards the King, and the courtiers moved into positions of protection. But the King had control of the stage, and in a moment he was practising a little torment on his antagonists: 'When the King extends a downturned forefinger with a cool "we license your departure" and Northumberland and Hotspur reluctantly fall to their knees before they leave, no further detail is necessary: a whole picture of court procedure springs up' (*Financial Times*, 25 April 1975). Then the King began to depart, until he thought of the coin, and came back to retrieve it 'in a rapid, shuffling return at the end of the scene' (David, 1978, p. 199).

This was certainly memorable behaviour, but to some it did not seem exactly royal, not at all like the Bolingbroke of *Richard II* or the Henry IV who is so conscience-stricken that he wants to undertake a pilgrimage to Jerusalem. Yet James did not overlook the Bolingbroke of the earlier play or the Henry IV of history in his preparation for the role. He just interpreted them differently by insisting that the characteristics discovered in his study would have to be connected to the element the actor has to work with on the stage, the words he has to speak. The King's words in this play are harsh, James found. 'Phrases like "intestine shock" are marvellous,' he said in an interview with Michael Mullin, referring to the opening speech of the play:

> No more shall trenching war channel her fields,
> Nor bruise her flow'rets with the armed hoofs
> Of hostile paces. Those opposed eyes
> Which, like the meteors of a troubled heaven,
> All of one nature, of one substance bred,
> Did lately meet in the intestine shock
> And furious close of civil butchery ... (I. i. 7-13)

'That's where civil war hurts: brother against brother, man against man,' James went on. 'It's an affront to society – an intestine shock, civil butchery. The whole speech is full of interesting words. He's a man for instance who talks not of *flowers*, but *flow'rets* – somehow a harsher, harder word, a word used by somebody who doesn't often talk or think about flowers, except as underfoot in a battlefield' (Mullin, p. 23). The aggressiveness of the words, together with the very element reviewers couldn't find in the performance, the prior history of Bolingbroke, gave James the idea of a Henry IV who had battled for all of his gains and still found himself out of place. 'He knows that he doesn't cut it as a king, that the charisma of kingship hasn't come easily to him. It has to be worked for.' His relationship with his son is strained because he has learned to repress his emotions. There are no women in his world at all, James noted, not in any of the three plays in which he appears. 'What's the difference between a household which contains a woman and a household that doesn't? One quite obvious thing is that very much less affection is shown.' And look at Henry's own father, John of Gaunt in *Richard II*. He says he spoke in favour of his son's banishment because he was acting as a counsellor and not as a father. So there is repression throughout Henry IV's background, and his treatment of Prince Hal is a continuation of the same sort of emotionless conditioning. 'Here's a man who hasn't learned how to handle his emotions and his solution to the problem is to suppress them completely. Except in moments of extreme stress. Then they come out' (Mullin, p. 22).

The contrast between James's turbulent interpretation and the restrained Falstaff of Brewster Mason was striking. With the King becoming volatile and unpredictable, Mason took Falstaff in the direction of stability. To some extent this was predetermined by Mason's Falstaff in *The Merry Wives of Windsor*, which he had first played in a Terry Hands production seven years earlier. This production was now being revived to join the other Falstaff plays of 1975, so Mason's task was to repeat his earlier success in the comedy and translate it into the history plays. In *The Merry Wives*, he had been notably successful in portraying Falstaff as a gentleman in decline. 'This Falstaff had dignity and a true if soiled knighthood', one critic wrote of the 1968 performance, more a 'victim of circumstances' than a figure of fun (Evans, 'The Reason Why', p. 139). Repeating this unorthodox approach proved manageable enough for the revived *Merry Wives*, but in taking up the histories Mason came upon the problem that the character of Falstaff varies with the genres in which he appears. In *1 Henry IV* it is hard to make Falstaff a gentleman. As we will see in Chapter VII, John Woodvine's Falstaff for the English Shakespeare Company in 1986 did accomplish this unlikely possibility, although his was a gentleman with a sneer and more than a hint of danger about him. Mason tried to make Falstaff amiable most of the time and even courageous on the battlefield: he startled everyone by *challenging* the redoubtable Douglas at Shrewsbury. It was certainly clear why Hal preferred the companionship of this surrogate Eastcheap father to the tantrums of his real father at Court. The trouble was that Mason had to underplay a part that teems with broad possibilities while James was ringing all the changes on a part that is supposed to be fairly predictable. Mason, judging by the reviews, came second. It was 'a dispiriting low-key performance' (*Guardian*, 25 April 1975), 'dignified but rarely funny' (Thomson, p. 154), and – for those who admired the performance – 'refreshing in its underemphasis' (Speaight, 'Shakespeare in Britain', p. 18).

The leading beneficiary of James's Henry was Alan Howard, who found that his own tendency towards unexpected psychological readings was being rivalled by the actor playing his father, of all people, and who thus had to rise to the challenge of unorthodoxy as a matter of Oedipal necessity. The real triumph for Howard was *Henry V*, of course, by which time *he* was the King, and Emrys James was celebrating him in the role of the Chorus. Sons usually have the advantage in the long run. Within *1 Henry IV*, Howard found his best opportunity for surprising innovation in the famous tavern scene, when he was apart from his father. This did not occur on the line other Hals had made their speciality. 'I do, I will' Howard delivered in what has become the traditional way by now, with fierce deliberateness. But he prepared for this line with an earlier surprise. He had, until the tavern scene, been a more relaxed Hal than is usual since Burton – even 'too self-consciously tow-haired and boyish' for one reviewer (*Guardian*, 25 April 1975). With Mason's Falstaff he could be at ease, even cuddling up to him a bit, a gesture impossible to offer his father. Small pleasures were his to enjoy – pleasures like the sensuousness of words: 'witness the dreamy relish of "the blessed sun himself a fair hot wench in flame cloured taffeta"' (David, 1978, p. 199). Drink was another pleasure: this Hal had a goblet in his hand at every opportunity. His 'I know you all' soliloquy was more innocent than is usual, 'more a good resolution than a real plan of action' (*The Times*, 25 April 1975).

Behind these signs of warmth and pleasure, Howard kept the beat of the Hal that would have to break out eventually. The change came when no one expected it. In the tavern scene, Falstaff talks of the northern rebellion and asks Hal if he is afraid: ' But tell me, Hal, art not thou horrible afeard? Thou being heir apparent, could the world pick thee out three such enemies again as that fiend Douglas, that spirit Percy, and that devil Glendower? Art thou not horribly

afraid?' (II. iv. 354-5). Normally Hal's answer is chipper and teas-
ing: 'Not a whit, i'faith. I lack some of thy instinct.' He has been
playing his elaborate joke on Falstaff, after all, and is at the top of
his form. But Alan Howard's Hal could not answer the first 'art not
thou horrible afeard?' He *was* afraid. The tavern crowd crept closer
to him during his pause, knowing something was wrong. Falstaff
named the fied Douglas, the spirit Percy, the devil Glendower, and
asked about fear again. Hal flung away from them to the other side
of the stage, and finally managed 'not a whit' in a voice fraught with
worry.

From that point to the end of the tavern scene, Hal became
increasingly animated and determined to face down his fear. The
rest of the scene was focused on his need to control himself and his
surroundings. When it came his turn to play the King, he was
taking command of the tavern as though it was becoming his own
theatre. A runway of five barrels in increasing height was set up by
the drawers, for Hal to ascend to the tavern table, where a preview
of the eventual rejection of Falstaff was acted out. On Falstaff's
'banish plump Jack, and banish all the world', Hal stood up from his
chair and shook the mock-crown from his head. Suddenly everyone
knelt, except Falstaff. (In the eventual rejection in *Part Two*, with
Howard now all in gold, Falstaff was the only one who did kneel, on
'Fall to thy prayers, old man.') Here he gained a 'chilling authority'
for the reviewer who had found him too boyish before. 'You actually see the growing moral disgust for his old drinking companion'
(*Guardian*, 25 April 1975). Thus Howard surprised everyone with a
fearful Hal, then used the rest of the tavern scene for the broad
theatricality of his self-assertion. Not every reviewer admired this
manoeuvre, it must be admitted. 'The emphasis here was altogether
too great,' wrote one. 'If at this early juncture the words are seen not
merely to strike a chill in Falstaff but to freeze the whole company
at the inn, the subtlety of the effect is destroyed' (David, 1978, p.
197).

Two neurotics, then, father and son, were the heart of the 1975
production, perhaps not quite convincing some in the audience
who thought the royal family should be nicer. The anti-heroism of
the 1964 interpretation was now being intensified in the domestic
psychology upon which the 1975 production was based, and even
those who were offended by the extremity of the interpretations
admitted the intelligence of the effort. Emrys James and Alan
Howard were establishing an anxious coherence in the relationship

of the father and son, for as one watched James's outlandishly strident behaviour, one knew that this is what Alan Howard's Hal was likely to become if he merely stayed at Court and tussled with his father. James observed that in all three plays in which he was involved, Bolingbroke / King Henry is absorbed by political calculations: his performance showed what Alan Howard was well on the way to showing too, that if this is the single dimension of a life, the life will be badly twisted. Thus one could read the other characters against James's controversial performance and see that Mason's understated Falstaff and the rest of the Boar's Head crowd were not just a contrast to the Court but an antidote necessary if Hal was not to travel his father's route towards an emotional breakdown.

* * *

The problem with the 1975 production was not in Emrys James's performance, or Alan Howard's, nor was it a fault of Terry Hands' direction. This *1 Henry IV* was intelligent and coherent, the kind of production that can prove eye-opening to anyone new to the play and provocative to the veterans as well. The problem in 1975 lay with the cycle itself. It had by now become necessary to think in terms of history cycles at the RSC, but it was also necessary to think freshly about them, and the fresh thinking of 1975 really centred not on a cycle but on *Henry V* itself. Beginning with the rehearsal device and building the company into a 'band of brothers' by the time of the Battle of Agincourt is a brilliant one-play device, but *1 Henry IV* is another play. I have mentioned that a great deal of thought went into making connections between the two plays, and the carry-over of ideas about role-playing and theatricality from their origin in *Henry V* to their application in *1 Henry IV* produced real innovation. One can also detect signs of strain, however, particularly in the abundance of commentary by which the RSC surrounded the production.

Take Ronald Bryden, for example. In 1964, when everyone was caught up by Peter Hall's treatment of the history cycle, Bryden was one reviewer who held out against the basic idea that Prince Hal/ Henry undergoes maturity and character development. In challenging Peter Hall's conception of the cycle, Bryden wrote that Shakespeare 'made no atttempt to explain the changes by which ... the wild Prince Hal turned into a chivalrous monarch' (*New Statesman*, 24 April 1964). By 1975 Bryden was seeing things differently, perhaps from the fresh perspective of his position as 'Play Advisor' to the RSC. He announced in a programme note for the new cycle that 'the two parts of *Henry IV* and *Henry V* form a trilogy about the education of a king', and the elaborateness of the argument that followed showed there was nothing half-hearted about this new conviction. Raising the possibility that Shakespeare invented the *Bildungsroman*, Bryden wrote, 'Prince Hal is the first of that long line of young men whose educations for manhood have been the subject of European masterpieces – Goethe's Wilhelm Meister, Stendhal's Julien Sorel, Dickens' David Copperfield, Thackeray's Pendennis.'

This invigorating piece of literary history seems intended for the same effect as Terry Hands' comment, quoted earlier, about Shakespeare's preference for psychology of kingship over the 'shallow science' of politics. These plays are about the making of a king, and although that assertion would seem to be rife with the political (Bryden, for example, suggested that Shakespeare saw Henry V's achievement as parallel to the Tudor establishment in the reign of Henry VII), it is always possible to claim something 'timeless' about a young man's struggle to grow up, something essential to male nature itself and thus untainted by the contingencies of the political. The stage 'is always the blank slate on which life writes its lessons for Henry,' Bryden's programme note goes on to say, ' the bare, metaphysical arena in which the soul of a royal Everyman discovers his destiny and true friends. Shakespeare's "histories" do not take place in time, in the usual sense of chronology.'

There is no reason why the political and the psychological *have* to be separated, when one stops to think about it, and the 1975 repudiation of politics as 'shallow', along with the detection of a *Bildungsroman* psychology in Shakespeare deep enough for Stendhal and Goethe, seems to be either a defence against an attack which no one was actually mounting or an effort to find a new justification for cycle-thinking that was growing tired.

There was, that is to say, a sense of strain behind the 1975 *1 Henry IV*, a sense of strain more apparent in the effort to link this production to a cycle than in the production itself. I have quoted a member of the royal family who compared the 'band of brothers' at Agincourt to the financial supporters of the RSC. The imaginative challenge offered by this comparison is to be welcomed from a royal consort, but one reads even more closely when one discovers much the same thing being said by the Artistic Director of the theatre itself. Here is Trevor Nunn, doing his own version of the St

Crispin's Day speech: 1975 was 'a year, in fact, for stiffening the sinews, conjuring up the blood and imitating the action of a tiger. All of which seemed one more reason for celebrating the centenary by performing a cycle of Shakespeare's *Henry IV, Parts One and Two, Henry V* and his other Falstaff play, *The Merry Wives of Windsor.*' The reason for fighting at Agincourt in 1415 and the reason for doing a cycle at Stratford in 1975 are somehow to be linked, and the phrase that is to push this comparison along without anyone noticing is 'celebrating the centenary'. Everyone was celebrating the centenary at Stratford, and it follows that a cycle of histories would be staged. Yet the logic that brings a cycle out of a centenary is hardly self-evident, nor does it appear that this was really a centenary. Those who counted found it had actually been but ninety-six years since the first play was staged by the Stratford company. The centenary of what, then? If one looked across the necessary 100 years to 1875, one found that the planning group for the Stratford company had been called together in that year. So in 1975 the tiger was being imitated in celebration of a committee being formed.

These proclamations were not scandalous. Everyone knew what was going on. The company was in trouble and some quick footwork was necessary to get free of it. Political image making was alive in the company that said its plays were not political, and a bit of the flim-flam was understandable in the company's pronouncements. At the same time something more serious was occurring, in the degeneration of motives for staging a history cycle at the RSC. The 1951 cycle had its political rationale too, as part of the post-war strategy for asserting the strength of British culture, and of course it was intended to make money, but no one had to scrabble up the victory at Agincourt as a reason for what was being undertaken. That cycle was the exploration of a new idea in the modern Shakespearian theatre, and thus it had an artistic validity by which the productions could be organised, staged, advertised, and explained. By 1975, no one could find the artistic motive for doing a cycle in the first place. That is, I assume, why the RSC had some trouble deciding just what the cycle was. The *Merry Wives of Windsor* that was revived after seven years was being brought back to make what some were willing to call a Falstaff cycle. The programme note in 1975 tried to justify this by calling upon Shakespeare's intentions: 'it is arguable that the comedy grew out of the histories because, in Shakespeare's mind at least, the Elizabethan merchant class of *The Merry Wives* were the children of Henry V's achievement at Agincourt'. Agincourt again! If that were true, it would justify 'Philip's' claim that by giving money to the RSC the merchant class of today could join the St Crispin's Day band of brothers.

But no one took the programme note seriously about the reason for including *The Merry Wives*, and before long a cycle of another sort was in the planning, for Alan Howard's success as Henry V raised hopes that a *Henry VI* with him in the title role would be joined to *Henry V*, and when this was accomplished in Howard's next Stratford season, 1977, the idea was taking hold that he should do more kings. By 1980 he had added Richard II and Richard III to his royal repertory. This series was solidly based on Howard's achievement as Henry V, but it left hanging the question of why the *Henry IV* plays were done at all in 1975.

The answer to that question must include the recognition that *1 Henry IV* and the various kinds of cycles to which it can be said to belong have become part of the duller institutional thinking at the RSC. In part this is financial thinking. Cycles can be counted on to make money. They use the same set and many of the same costumes for more than one play. They have popular appeal and, in the interests of transmitting Shakespeare's version of English history, a certain power to draw school parties. But institutional routine is also ceremonial. More than any other play, *1 Henry IV* is swung into position on occasions of dignity and ceremony in Stratford. It has always been used that way. It was chosen to open the new Stratford Memorial Theatre itself in 1932, on Shakespeare's birthday. It was the birthday play during the 1951 cycle. In 1964, in productions that challenged many of the traditional views of the histories, this one tradition remained intact: *1 Henry IV* was the birthday play again. The 1975 season played a trim variation by calling 26 April the birthday and staging its best production, *Henry V*, on that date, but those Stratford pilgrims who knew the traditional date of the birthday and accordingly attended the theatre on 23 April would have seen the real birthday play, which was again *1 Henry IV*. So during the centenary which was not truly a centenary, *1 Henry IV* was scheduled for the birthday which was not precisely the birthday, as part of a cycle that was not exactly the Falstaff cycle, not really the English history cycle, and not yet the Alan Howard-as-King cycle.

Glance ahead to 1982, when the new London theatre so long

[85]

sought by the RSC finally opened at the Barbican. This was part of the future which was ensured for the company by the financial success of their 1975 season. It perhaps goes without saying that the first Shakespearian productions at the Barbican were another cycle of histories and that the birthday play was again *1 Henry IV*. I am more concerned to report that Trevor Nunn announced *six years earlier*, in 1976, that a history cycle would open the new theatre (Beauman, *Henry V*, p. 8). The thinking at the RSC had become so accustomed to taking the *Henrys* as curtain-raisers for occasions of wealth and power that the venture could be predicted before some of the actors in the eventual production were out of secondary school.

That is what Falstaff has come to at last. The institutional theatre has enclosed him with cycles. I have presented this as the major shift in modern productions of *1 Henry IV*. The theatre of our time has changed the older emphasis on star turns for the actors of Falstaff and Hotspur to a new concentration on the political career of Prince Hal and his relationship to the two older figures in his life, his father and Falstaff. This change of emphasis was largely created in the Stratford productions of 1951 and 1964, but it has now lost its artistic rationale and become a routine assumption at the theatre that nourished it originally. Now the young hero is primarily a study in character disorder. He needs to develop. In 1982, at the Barbican, Gerald Murphy's Prince Hal had more developing to do than the others, because he started from an especially low point of childish resentfulness. Some reviewers wondered if he actually did develop. But development was the issue in any case, and this production was praised for having even more 'depth-psychology' than did the Hands version. It is said to have 'touches of Freud, Dickens, Tolstoy', and to be 'about a Prince symbolically caught between two fathers' (Michael Billington, quoted in Trussler, 1982-83, p. 7).

The excitement and innovation of the 1975 production, that is to say, occurred as part of the RSC's downgrading of the political in the interpretation of the history plays, and this tendency carried through to the 1982 cycle, which helped to celebrate the opening of the Barbican. The history plays were being used to solve problems during these years, problems of the growing deficit in 1975 and of the Barbican expenses in 1982. The 1975 deficit was turned to a surplus, but the Barbican expenses proved recalcitrant and could not be matched by such measures as the RSC's growing dependence on corporate sponsorship, musicals intended for long runs in the West End and on Broadway, higher ticket prices, and increases (not enough, of course, and still not as much as the National's) in the government subsidy. Even a further dose of history-cycle in 1989, the early histories this time, failed to prevent what the corporate support, the popular musicals, and higher ticket prices also failed to prevent, the closing down of the RSC's Barbican operation for the winter season of 1990.

The strain and nervousness of the RSC commentary surrounding the 1975 cycle can best be explained as administrative thinking that puts finance and public relations ahead of artistry and then is hard-pressed to pretend that the artistry comes first. The most peculiar aspect of the commentary – the claim that these obviously political history plays are to be understood as non-political – I take to be the manoeuvring of an administration looking for safety and finding it in the 'depth-psychology' of adolescent male experience. So long as Prince Hal is said to be caught up in such timeless and essential experience, his career will seem purified of the political and all the more agreeable to the managers of our affairs. But the theatre that survives on the basis of such thinking will be timid in its artistic planning and beggarly in its financial appeals to the wealthy and powerful.

CHAPTER VI

Film and television
1966. *Chimes at Midnight*: Orson Welles
1979. BBC Television: Cedric Messina and David Giles

While the Royal Shakespeare Company was mounting their various cycles of history plays, Orson Welles was working in the opposite direction. He was gathering all the Falstaff plays and condensing them into a single production, which eventually resulted in his two-hour film of 1966, *Chimes at Midnight*.

Before that, Welles had been working on Falstaff scripts for years, drawing together the basic episodes of *1* and *2 Henry IV* and adding pieces from *Henry V* and *The Merry Wives of Windsor*. He had started with a stage play called *Five Kings*, a one-evening compilation of the *Henrys* which was produced unsuccessfully in America in 1938. In 1960 he tried another stage compilation of the histories for the Gate Theatre in Dublin. This was the first version actually called *Chimes at Midnight*, and it was abandoned before its projected tour to the Continent and London. The film opportunity arose in 1964, when Welles convinced a producer that he would make *Treasure Island* on location in Spain, then filmed *Chimes at Midnight* instead. In all three versions, he was not interested in the historical epic formed by the histories; he was interested in Falstaff – or, perhaps more accurately, in a certain angle of vision which can be thought of as Falstaffian.

* * *

One sign of the Falstaffian undertaking is that the film version of *Chimes at Midnight* freely plunders and rearranges the underlying Shakespeare texts. Here, for example, is Welles' rendition of the first episode between Falstaff and Hal, I. ii, the scene which editors usually place in 'a room in Hal's house' and which productions usually begin with Falstaff awakening after heavy slumber. (The original text has merely '*Enter the Prince of Wales and Sir John Falstaff*', followed by Falstaff's line, 'Now, Hal, what time of day is it, lad?') In Welles' film the scene begins with a close-up of a pot of ale, then the camera moves back to reveal the drinker as Hal. The camera backtracks further to reveal a room in the Boar's Head, and the first sequence has Hal moving out of that room, up some stairs, into another room and up some more stairs – Welles had constructed an entire Boar's Head Tavern in a Madrid warehouse under the pretence that it would be the Admiral Benbow Inn in *Treasure Island*. The sequence is wordless motion, but the aim of the motion (and of the film) is to search for a missing Falstaff.

Falstaff is asleep in another room, where Hal's search stops. Poins appears and announces that he has picked the old man's pocket and has filched a tavern reckoning from him. So the scene really takes its beginning from the end of II. iv, the famous tavern scene, where Shakespeare has a sleeping Falstaff having his pockets picked. But then the film has Falstaff awaken to the beginning of the actual first scene with Hal, I. ii, interspersed with some parts of Act III, where Falstaff complains to the Hostess that he has been robbed. Bits then appear from *Henry V* and *The Merry Wives* before a return to II. iv and the taunting of Falstaff over the tavern reckoning (two gallons of sack to a half-pennyworth of bread – in this version he owes the Hostess for these things) which has been picked from his pocket. This blends into another snatch of III. iii before it returns to I. ii and the plan that is laid for the Gadshill robbery. The scene works its way to a conclusion centred on the 'I know you all' soliloquy, which is Shakespeare's ending of I. ii, but Hal delivers the speech with Falstaff standing behind him, rendering questionable the speech's normal function as a soliloquy. The ending foregrounds Falstaff at the tavern entrance, with Hal departing towards a castle which can be seen in the distance.

Throughout his career, Welles was able to combine brilliance and nonsense as though the two were a perfect fit. The brilliance of *Chimes at Midnight* lies in its shots of wordless movement, where editing and composition create a cinematic accomplishment that Shakespeare could not have envisioned. The movement through the Boar's Head in the sequence outlined above has that kind of energy and nerve, and the business of looking for Falstaff – 'Where's

Falstaff?' is Hal's first line, as he moves through one of the rooms – is a visual metaphor of the film's central idea. Falstaff is not exactly there. Even when he is found and is filling the screen, 'Where's Falstaff' is one of the puzzles. Welles keeps Falstaff at the centre of the frame as often as he can, but only in the paradoxical interest of showing his displacement. He is there so often because the film aims for his absence.

The shadow of rejection is cast over Falstaff from the beginning, and Hal never acts as though their relationship could reach any other conclusion. To put the pickpocket business first is to make Falstaff vulnerable to Hal's manipulations before he has even a word to say for himself. And when he does have a word to say for himself, Welles tends to mumble and downplay Falstaff's best speeches, not just in this first tavern scene but all the way through. Welles had entered the 'throwaway' phase of his career by the time he made this film, whereby he addressed the problem of his deep, penetrating, colourless voice by refusing to let the audience hear very much of what it was saying. One reason *Chimes at Midnight* received poor reviews at first was its refusal to deliver what every-one expected to be the primary value, the famous Falstaff lines. Bosley Crowther's review was typical: 'Mr. Welles' basso profundo speech, which he seems to direct toward his innards instead of out through his lips, makes it all the more difficult to catch the drift of this great, bearded, untidy man who waddles and cocks his hairy eyebrows and generally bluffs his way through the film' (*New York Times*, 20 March 1967).

What passed unnoticed in the initial reviews was the possibility that distinct speech might be under some sort of deliberate chal-lenge in this film. The possibility was certainly there from the start, for the one actor who can always be understood is John Gielgud, playing a distant, unloving King Henry IV through the flute-like tones of his famous voice. If there are two father-figures for Hal, with the negative one speaking his famous lines beautifully and the valorised one throwing them away, perhaps our usual preconcep-tions about dramatic speech are being deliberately challenged. Certainly Gielgud's voice is a subject of the film itself, for both Falstaff and Hal parody it perfectly in the play-acting scene. By contrast, Welles' Falstaff fills the screen while his voice turns inaudible – a huge Falstaff being devoiced.

The handling of Hal's 'I know you all' speech at the end of the sequence outlined above is an example of Falstaff's displacement.

In Shakespeare, the monologue has a startling effect because Hal has just been acting the reprobate and now he says he is only pretending. He has agreed to join the Gadshill robbery. He has been acting like the legendary Hal, madcap and prodigal. Everyone knows the legendary Hal. He was truly the scapegrace as a young man, then he went through a wondrous reformation and became a great king. Shakespeare sets up that expectation only to snatch it away in the surprising soliloquy – Hal is only pretending to be the scapegrace so as to bring about his reformation on his own schedule. He will create his own legend. It is essential to the Shakespearian surprise that the audience be informed about motives unknown to everyone else in the play. That is why Shakespeare wrote a soliloquy – to give the audience advance notice of something important about Hal.

Welles changed this emphasis by holding Falstaff in the background and having Hal speak the soliloquy aloud, in a sort of reverie. Does Falstaff overhear the speech? According to the shooting script for the film, he 'half overhears' it (Hapgood, p. 46), and this intention seems especially clear when Hal turns to Falstaff and even gives him a wink on 'My reformation glittering o'er my fault, / Shall show more goodly and attract more eyes / Than that which hath no foil to set it off' (I. ii. 201-3, Lyons, p. 52). But one cannot be sure what Falstaff hears, if anything, and it is the very uncertainty that creates the new effect. One way or the other, Falstaff is being manipulated. He is either being left out because he doesn't hear or insulted because he does. The speech is no longer an isolated surprise about Hal and his political calculations. It is now an address being brought to bear on Falstaff, whether he hears it or not. Welles refuses to register any reaction as he stands in the background. He seems to be listening, but why does he show no reaction? He just stands there, as though he is not quite acting, giving a different version of his throwaway manner of speech. It does not matter whether he hears. It matters that his presence in the background has a blank aspect to it. Absence is already the figure he cuts.

But the blank aspect of this background figure is also supposed to draw sympathy. In the long run, Welles gains brilliant results by displacing his centralised Falstaff and devaluing the Shakespeare text, but there is a price to be paid in the short run, and the price is the sentimentality of the background figure of 'I know you all.' He is either being left out or insulted, and the undecidability is a fine stroke, but the episode is set up for us to feel *sorry* for him in either case. Falstaff has tried to be charming to Hal a minute before. The scene has been rearranged so that we have just heard Falstaff's routine on 'Let us be Diana's foresters, gentlemen of the shade, minions of the moon, men of good government, being governed, as the sea is, by our noble and chaste mistress the moon, under whose countenance we steal', moved in from the beginning of the Shakespearian scene. I have earlier mentioned that in the 1951 production Anthony Quayle used the first three phrases of this speech with increasingly extravagant gestures in order to win a laugh from Richard Burton's sullen Hal. It was part of Falstaff's joviality. Shifting these lines so that they become a prelude for Hal's reverie creates an easy sentiment. Hal is now meditating his political scheme even as Falstaff is being rhetorically charming. How could Hal be so callous? This effect is repeated at the end of the reverie, where Falstaff calls 'I prithee, sweet wag, shall there be gallows standing in England when thou art king?' as Hal is leaving him and heading for the castle in the distance. Again it is difficult to understand how such a charming piece of drollery can be left behind. Rejection is already taking place.

If Welles combined brilliance and nonsense, we are now looking at the nonsense. In an interview with Juan Cobos and Miguel Rubio shortly after *Chimes at Midnight* was released, Welles was pleased to note that on four separate occasions Prince Hal actually leaves Falstaff and heads in the direction of the castle of his father, and the viewer will not be able to doubt that this does indeed happen. Four little rejections lead up to one big rejection, and always the goal is the castle. 'The farewell is performed about four times during the movie, foreshadowed four times' – Welles was relentless on this point (Lyons, p. 261). The end of 'I know you all' is the first of the four. In the same interview, Welles announced that the film was intended 'as a lament ... for the death of Merrie England,' Merrie England being 'the age of chivalry, of simplicity, of Maytime and all that'. One must suppose that Falstaff and the Boar's Head Tavern were the centre of this Merrie England, although it is hard to see what the tavern episodes outlined above have to do with chivalry and simplicity, let alone 'Maytime and all that'.

Hotspur is sometimes regarded as the representative of 'the age of chivalry', but Welles could not mean *his* Hotspur this way, for his Hotspur is treated to a good deal of larking: he reads his letter at the beginning of II. iii sitting in a wooden tub of water, with two suits of armour and racks of lances standing nearby, and throughout the scene his every move is intercut with trumpeters swivelling their horns on the ramparts of the castle (he loses his bath towel and reveals his buttocks on 'That roan shall be my throne' [II. iii. 67, Lyons, p. 56], then two trumpet bells are shown swinging into position side by side, to look like buttocks). If this Hotspur was Merrie England, it gets snickered out of existence early in the film.

The lament for Merrie England has to be a lament for Falstaff, vulnerable to the Prince from the beginning, ripe for rejection – this Falstaff who was in Welles' opinion 'the greatest conception of a good man, the most completely good man, in all drama' (Lyons, p. 261). To connect Falstaff with chivalry, simplicity, and goodness is about as accurate as celebrating 'Maytime and all that' in a film notable for its winter landscapes. And the film about Merrie England was shot in Spain.

Fortunately, the brilliance is always evident too. It can be seen, for example, in technical details such as the lighting. This is a black-and-white film wondrous with light – daylight, a cold sun in a Spanish winter, nothing to do with Maytime in Merrie England. In the castle of Henry IV, beams of light angle down from high windows and streak across the cold greys and shadows of the royal Court, in contrast to the Gadshill robbery scene, where diffused light (an effect created by burning incense) filters through the trees. When it comes to making location lighting count for something, Welles is a genius, but his rearrangement of 'I know you all' shows the need for mere pathos breaking through again. There is 'lighting' there too, but this is symbolic lighting. Falstaff's lines about being minions of the moon, thanks to the repositioning, are now set directly against Hal's soliloquy about the sun. By casting off Falstaff, Hal says, he will please everyone like the sun coming out from behind the clouds. The heavy hand of significance even directs Hal to look up towards the sun as he speaks. He is the royal son looking at the natural sun – does everybody get it? – and Falstaff has just said that he lives by the changeable moon. This is lamentable pedantry. Manipulating the text so as to get Falstaff's moon cuddled up against Hal's sun in the soliloquy is like the arch condescension of having Hal leave Falstaff for the castle four times in order to foreshadow the rejection. This is sometimes a children's film.

* * *

[93]

The repeated 'rejections' of Falstaff described above are merely the film-maker's version of a point originally learned in the theatre. Ralph Richardson made the pathos of Falstaff's rejection vivid in 1945, and the Stratford cycle of 1951 turned pathos into political necessity: Falstaff must be rejected for the good of the realm. Welles works both of these veins, but the importance of *Chimes at Midnight* lies in discoveries that cannot be made in the theatre, discoveries of the film-medium itself. The film matters because of its composition of movement and its rhythm of editing. *Chimes at Midnight* can be watched with pleasure by turning off the sound and following the motion on the screen for its own sake, an experiment that would have the advantage of silencing the awful soundtrack, with its failure of synchronisation in the first reel and its disembodied dubbing (the entire film was dubbed later, with Welles doing a number of the minor voices himself). By getting rid of what offended Bosley Crowther, one is left with the opportunity to *see* the film, and to recognise that spoken language is far from its primary value.

The gradual increase of appreciation for *Chimes at Midnight* has occurred in part because this possibility – that the spoken text is deliberately subordinated to the visual – has been recognised and explored. To a generation that thought Olivier's way of making Shakespeare films was the right and only way, *Chimes at Midnight* seemed exasperating and primitive; but the generation whose values were formed in the late 1960s and the 1970s, when language itself was placed under sceptical and paradoxical questioning, was prepared to see this film in a new way and to understand that one of its effects was to challenge the usual technique in Shakespeare films. By 1984 Dudley Andrew was able to make this point comfortably:

> Some viewers find it maddening to find our greatest poet left to the mercy of Welles with his bizarre sense of sound mixing and of pace. They prefer the Olivier films where every speech is directed to the audience, amplified by the closed shell of its decor, separated from neighboring speeches by studied silences if not actual changes in camera setup. ... In contrast, Welles violated the sanctity of the manuscript, piecing and patching a single film from the fragments of five different plays. Instead of a *text* which comfortingly remains behind the scenes and outlasts the film, Welles gives us a *voice* disconcertingly disappearing over time. ... Far from betraying theatre, cinema here bestows upon it a most intimate gift, to let its cultured speeches contend with the wind of a truly open space. (*Film in the Aura of Art*, pp. 165-6)

[94]

What is best about that perception is its metaphor of a 'truly open space', which includes Welles' Spanish locations not as a stand-in for Merrie England but as places where visual rhythms occur. In the same interview in which Welles prattled on about Merrie England, he made this penetrating comment: 'what I am trying to do is to see the outside, real world through the same eyes as the inside fabricated one'. This unity between inside and outside would have to be attempted through Falstaff, not on the understanding that Falstaff is a famous character with famous lines about 'honour' and the like, but on the understanding that Falstaff is the camera. You do not merely 'play' Falstaff in a film, Welles said, you 'make a world' for him (Lyons, p. 260). That is what the camera does. It makes a world for the line of vision in the film, a line of vision that lets one 'see the outside, real world through the same eyes as the inside fabricated one'. There is no real outside world in the film that is not connected to the vision of a fabricated world. Those impressive locations in Spain form a composition for Falstaff – not exactly the world as seen through his eyes, rather the world that enables his eyes, which are different from ordinary eyes, to see.

If anyone is the camera, of course, it is Welles himself. His identification with Falstaff lies along a line of vision. The unity of inside and outside that he sought is a unity between the Falstaff he played and the camera he guided – especially if one weighs into the equation the subterfuges and improvisations Welles had to employ in order to do the film at all: not just getting the money to build his own Boar's Head Tavern in Spain by telling his producer it would be the Admiral Benbow Inn in the *Treasure Island* he was promising to make, but also dressing Prince Hal in a leather tunic first worn by Jayne Mansfield in *The Sheriff of Fractured Jaw*, also shot in Spain (Lyons, p. 280), or dealing with the departure of Gielgud after the first four weeks of shooting by using a double for Henry IV's striking entrance in the battle scene, where only the bottom of his robe is visible. If Falstaff had made films, he would have made something like this one.

The locations are spaces where visual rhythms occur. Only along straight lines does King Henry IV (Gielgud) move through his vast stony palace, passing ranks of soldiers and courtiers on his way to a throne raised on a square platform. Sunlight pours in from windows high beyond reach, and the beams are separated so that one can virtually see the crenellations in the windows. Nothing bends in this court, but in Falstaff's locations all motion is curved and wayward. The Boar's Head Tavern is itself a panoply of entrances, passageways, windows, bedrooms, and balconies through, around, and under which people dart, run, twist, duck. No one just walks anywhere. Keith Baxter, who played Hal, said that the camera track at the tavern was laid on an S, 'and the actors as well as the camera were made to move in very intricate ways' (Lyons, p. 270).

The highlight at the Boar's Head is not the play-acting of Falstaff and Hal, as it is in the modern theatre, but the aftermath, when the sheriff is coming in and everyone scatters. Welles delivers seventeen shots of motion without a line of dialogue, creating a disorderly, vibrant world in motion more fully than could be done in words. The first several shots run this way in the printed script (numbers are the shot numbers in Lyons):

365 ... Behind the Prince in the background women run along the balcony and there is a general commotion.
366 ... The Hostess is running out of the shot at right, followed by young women who run toward the camera and scatter in various directions.
367 Falstaff and the Prince stand in front of the 'throne'; Falstaff holds the Prince by both arms. [This is actually the aftermath of the 'I do, I will' moment, which Keith Baxter's Hal has made very deliberate, but Falstaff's reaction has been interrupted by the outbreak of movement. Now, in passing, it is clear that he has reacted by gripping Hal's arms, but the gesture is caught in the fluidity of the tavern in motion. It is noticeable, but only as part of business that does not care about significant moments. There is no time for sentiment here – the sheriff is coming.] The camera tracks briefly, passing behind a post and then reframing the two men. The Prince turns away from him and jumps up on the table. Women run past them from right to left, both in the foreground and background.
368 ... the Prince, framed by two beams, leaps from the table between the beams and toward the camera. The camera, now level with the Prince, pans with him as he swings around one of the posts and runs down a balcony corridor.
369 ... Bardolph runs under the overhang of the balcony, followed by Peto. (Lyons, pp. 98-9)

This is just the beginning. In the midst of all the motion, at shot 378, Falstaff is discovered standing still – then he turns in a complete circle, as though it were necessary to respond to the pattern of movement, or as though he is the camera.

In the brilliant part of his interview about *Chimes at Midnight*, where he spoke of making an external world to accord with the inner perception of such a character as Falstaff, Welles went on to an incisive note about visual form: 'With me, the visual is a solution to what the poetical and musical form dictates' (Lyons, p. 263).

The battle scene in *Chimes at Midnight* is probably the fullest example of that idea in all of Welles' films. It is nearly ten minutes of sheer visual warfare. No word of Shakespeare is spoken. The sound is martial brasses and drums, and sometimes a women's chorus trying to be heard through the screams of men, the neighing of horses, and the clashing of metal on metal. The sequence begins with knights in full armour being lowered on to their horses by ropes and pulleys – one after another, including Falstaff (who breaks the rope) – in a parody of the steed-mounting in Olivier's *Henry V*. Then follow shots of cavalry charges (again with an eye on Olivier and his handling of the French cavalry attack at Agincourt), a rank of mounted King's forces advancing, a rank of rebel forces coming the other way, the straight-line movement of the King's castle scenes transposed to the battlefield. Everything is clear, as though war could be followed by a careful camera. Once the sides meet, however, the shots begin to follow one another in increasing tempo and the two sides become impossible to distinguish. Riders are driven to the ground, horses stumble, foot-soldiers come at one another with maces, axes, and swords; eventually men are crawling over each other in mud so thick that they can only slug at each other and tremble. Kenneth Branagh's Agincourt scenes, in *his* film of *Henry V*, must derive from this sequence.

Welles thought of shooting the scenes so that 'every cut seemed to be a blow, a counterblow, a blow received, a blow returned' (Lyons, p. 264), but the cuts are not so mechanically connected to the violence as that. They have their own violent tempo, which becomes awfully rapid as the battle becomes awfully long. The frames can no longer contain proper images after a while. As the opposing sides become indistinguishable, parts of men's bodies and parts of wounded horses fill the frames in a synecdoche of brutality. Spain, it can be imagined, provided more than the locations for the film: these wartime agonies are Picasso's *Guernica* in motion.

Here, from the printed script, are eight consecutive shots (from over 200 in the battle sequence) as an example of the editing:

758 ... Two men in combat. One, back to camera, is already falling backward as the other moves to strike again. A figure passing immediately in front of the camera blacks out the image so that the actual blow is not seen. When the figure has passed, one soldier lies on the ground and the other, his club at the ready, turns and moves out of the shot to the left. The camera stays momentarily with the man on the ground, then pans quickly up and to the right to include some horsemen, one of whom

impales a soldier with his lance.

759 ... a rider in armor moves to the right. He suddenly throws up his arms and plunges off his horse toward the camera, which follows the beginning of his fall.

760 ... footsoldiers, silhouetted in combat. The foreground is dominated by a horse, lying on its side, twisting and writhing with an arrow in its side.

761 ... A series of horses, moving very close to the camera, initially block out any image. After the pass, two men in Long Shot are seen struggling, with a body lying on the ground next to them.

762 ... a horseman with lance moves to the right and away from the camera. He unseats another horseman riding toward him, striking him with the lance. As he then moves further into the background at the right, a foot soldier crosses the foreground to the left, only his head visible.

763 ... The head and shoulders of a man in armor, apparently on horseback, with his back to the camera in the lower foreground of the frame. Beyond him can be seen a rider with couched lance, approaching him. Other horsemen ride forward in the further background.

764 ... the head and shoulders of the man in armor, still back to camera, with his sword raised. He suddenly throws his arms in the air and spins toward the camera, as if struck.

765 ... a helmeted rider with a club raised in his hand. He turns in the saddle toward the camera, swinging the club as he does. (Lyons, pp. 157-8)

These wordless scenes are introduced by Falstaff's speech about 'honour': 'Can honor set to a leg? No. Or an arm? No. Or take away the grief of a wound? No. Honor hath no skill in surgery then? No. What is honor? Air.' ... (V. i. 131-2, Lyons, p. 142, which is the text quoted here). Again Welles rejects the convention of soliloquy. He speaks these famous lines directly to an unimpressed Hal, whose thoughts are all for the coming battle. This is another example of the displaced Falstaff. His most famous speech (slightly cut) is directed at Hal, but Hal is not listening. The disregarded speech leads to the wordless battle sequence, from which Falstaff is literally displaced. He hides from it, and is shown peering out from one bush or another several times, a spectator in grotesquely oversized armour. This is not the battle as Falstaff would 'see' it. He sees only a little. We see much more, but what we see is Falstaffian nevertheless, for this amazing camera work does externalise Falstaff's cynicism about honour. It is a vivid example of the co-ordination between inner perception and outer world that Welles sought throughout the film.

The conclusion is Falstaff's in another sense. After Hal kills Hotspur in single combat, Falstaff steals the body, brings it before Hal, and claims the prize for himself. All this follows Shakespeare closely enough, but then Welles makes the un-Shakespearian move of bringing the King into the scene during Falstaff's account of the hour he and Hotspur fought by Shrewsbury clock (this is where the double replaced Gielgud). The presence of the King changes the game Falstaff is playing. He is now telling the royal father that the royal son's claim of a victory over Hotspur is in effect a lie. There follow ten close-ups of faces – the Prince, the King (Gielgud now, not the double, in shots taken earlier), the Prince again, Falstaff, the King again. This wordless sequence shows the King waiting for Hal to call this a lie, Hal refusing to expose Falstaff, and Falstaff (in one of Welles' most expressive moments) wondering if he hasn't gone too far this time, and loving the possibility that he has. The King breaks the cycle of close-ups by taking his haughty leave (the double again, seen from the back): his son seems to have protected Falstaff once more, turning his real father and his real King aside.

But Hal has not quite done that. He has refuelled his father's mistrust of him and deferred their reconciliation, but he has not really joined Falstaff. For a moment it appears that he has, for Falstaff has moved over to a huge cask of wine that the soldiers have with them and has poured out a tankard for himself and one for Hal. They are drinking together, and Falstaff is delivering the soliloquy, wrenched out of its place in *Part Two*, on sherris-sack. But Hal has no time for such licentiousness. He walks away, once again heading in the direction of the castle, following his father. There he goes again, walking out on one of Falstaff's fine rhetorical moments – another of those four leavetakings. By the end of the speech, he is so far away that he cannot hear it. And in case we do not get the point (this is such a disappointment to report about the end of the stunning battle-sequence) he even lets his tankard drop to the ground before heading off after his father.

* * *

There is another version of *1 Henry IV* preserved for all to see – the television version, made as part of the BBC's project to film all of Shakespeare's plays between 1978 and 1985. It is notable for its Falstaff, for Anthony Quayle here takes on the role again after thirty years, this time subduing the metallic edge of artificiality that marked his performance in 1951 and offering a humanised Falstaff along conventional lines. His performance is notable chiefly for Falstaff's soliloquies. Where Welles spoke these to an uninterested Hal, who refused to let the comedy have its effect, Quayle looks straight into the camera in close-up and speaks to viewers in their living-rooms. He is the only one who does this. The rest of the characters are caught up in history, or at least such pretence at history as is possible in a BBC studio, but Falstaff transcends the barrier of time and confides in us. J. L. Styan once remarked that there are 'two spheres of intelligence in the play, determined by the proximity of the audience' (Styan, p. 75). He was thinking of stage performances, but Quayle's remarkable soliloquies in the television version are so clearly set off from the rest of the production that they become one sphere of intelligence in themselves.

The other sphere is the rest of the production, which is inferior to the Falstaff sphere. The rest of the production is devoted to what has become the standard cycle-interpretation, that Falstaff is dangerous and must be rejected. The BBC, venturing to film all of Shakespeare's plays, was not going to overlook the ambitiousness of cycle-thinking (they did the four plays from *Richard II* through *Henry V* with consistent casting and staging, under the direction of David Giles, then filmed the *Henry VI* plays and *Richard III* as a separate and very different kind of cycle, directed by Jane Howell). If cycle-thinking puts the realm and its rulers ahead of Falstaff, and if the performance of Falstaff puts him well ahead of the realm and its rulers, trouble is brewing. Quayle's assured performance as Falstaff is the strongest element of the production, and the separate 'sphere of intelligence' provided by his addresses to the audience happily interrupts the dutiful effort to capture history in the space of the television studio. He is in better control of the medium – and this makes Prince Hal's efforts to take better control of the kingdom seem second-rate.

Control of the medium leads to the main difference between the film and television versions. Where *Chimes at Midnight* achieves technical sophistication and daring, the BBC *1 Henry IV* settles for a naive assumption about television itself. The naive assumption is that television is a form of realism with the camera recording a fictional world as the viewer would see it too, if only the viewer were there. The camera thus tries to be neutral and let us see things for ourselves. Welles' comments about trying 'to see the outside, real world through the same eyes as the inside fabricated one' charges the camera with Falstaffian idiosyncrasy, and the resulting vision does not reflect a world, it creates one. No one has ever 'been there' to see a battle like the Welles Battle of Shrewsbury with its increasing fragmentation and pace. It is filmic in nature. No one has ever 'been there' to see a battle like any of the stage Battles of Shrewsbury from the productions described in other chapters of this book, for a battle in a theatre moves unexpectedly and violently across a real space, the space of the stage, and thus threatens to expand beyond that real space and enter the other available space, which is ours in the audience. It is not a question of 'realism' so much as a question of distances, and the distances are those of the theatre itself. But in a television studio, the Battle of Shrewsbury is going to reduce to a minor problem of focus if the camera is assumed to be an instrument of realism and if the audience is thought to be interested only in seeing things for themselves, and that is what happens in the BBC *1 Henry IV*. (Falstaff's soliloquies break this assumption; he fills the screen and looks at *us*.)

The director and the set designer (David Giles and Don Homfrey) both said the achievement of the battle scenes was finding the right narrow lens to keep a clear focus on Hotspur and Hal while necessarily blurring and flattening the rest of the studio set. A narrow lens keeps the individual combatants clear, Homfrey said, and 'reduces the depth of field. ... A character is in focus, but perhaps even six inches behind him is out of focus' (*Henry IV, Part I: The BBC TV Shakespeare*, p. 19). Thus the space in which the battle occurs becomes the space of the focused shot, with something blurred and flattened behind it. The result is that the men fight across no distance at all, and the foregrounding of the struggle is obviously intended for viewing on the small screen at home or in school. So there is no space of battle within the scene, as there is in Welles' film, and no space of battle between the screen and the (relatively) safe place of viewing, as there is in live theatre. In the annals of battle-representation, this televised version comes to very little, and cannot be taken with full seriousness by anyone other than narrow-lens makers.

The way to solve this technical problem is to abandon the assumption of photographic realism and use the camera as an instrument of distortion and dislocation. The real lessons for Shakespearian battle scenes on television are being taught in commercials, MTV videos, and sporting events, where experiments in unexpected camera angles, tracking patterns, colours, visual design, repetition, and cutting are being tried daily as part of the medium itself (Waller, p. 28). But the transfer of experience from these popular and commercial arenas to Shakespeare is not being made, largely because the producers of Shakespeare on television

[101]

are not willing to bridge what is supposed to be Low Culture with this particular form of the High.

The pressure for High Culture was operating on the BBC project from the beginning. *1 Henry IV* came fairly early in the series, while Cedric Messina was the producer; and in accordance with the tradition that had by now become entrenched at the RSC, Messina and David Giles did a cycle running from *Richard II* through *Henry V*. Given the original intentions of the BBC, there was no chance for experimentation. These plays were being filmed as a monument to Shakespeare and they were intended to last for all time. As one reviewer said, without irony: 'The task is to present Shakespeare not to audiences of a few hundred faithful but to millions both across the globe and down the ages to come' (*The Times*, 17 December 1979). The cultural imperialism of this attitude is striking. The British Empire had shrunk to the BBC studios by 1979, but the technology to be found there could send one phase of English culture, the Shakespearian phase, worldwide if only the job could be done *correctly*.

The lighting, for example, would have to be correct. Scholars have noticed that imagery of light and dark runs through *1 Henry IV*, and to the wonder of no one it turns out that sunlight is for the forces of good, moonlight for the others. To be correct, one would put the King and Prince in the sunlight, Falstaff and Hotspur in the moonlight, which is the alignment given in the text. I have mentioned the disappointing moment when Welles has the Prince look into the sunlight in his 'I know you all' soliloquy, an example of correctness in action, but I have also mentioned the strange and beautiful shimmering that sunlight takes on in the Gadshill robbery sequence in the same film, which correctness would film in moonlight. The BBC films the Gadshill robbery in painterly moonlight and gains the opportunity for moral dullness by filming the rebel forces in moonlight too, before the Battle of Shrewsbury. This lighting design is following the text quite properly. Falstaff thinks of himself as one of Diana's foresters, minions of the moon, and Hotspur talks of plucking honour from the pale-faced moon. Of *course* they operate at night.

So insistent is this drive for correct meaning that the BBC even created an impossibility. Both scenes at the rebel camp, IV. iii and V. ii, are given the moonlight treatment. But between them comes a scene for the royal forces where the time has to be morning according to the text: 'How bloodily the sun begins to peer / Above yon bosky hill!' (V. i. 1-2), says the King, his cheek turning ruddy under a furious BBC lamp. The trouble is that this is the morning of the battle, and there is no way in the logic of nature for the subsequent rebel scene to occur in moonlight (McMillin, pp. 76-7). The sun is up, we have seen it shining on royalty, and the rebels will be dead by nightfall. That the second rebel scene does occur at night must be owed to the logic of correctness, which wants one more contrast between the sunlight of royalty and the lunacy of rebellion. The logic of correctness is different from the logic of nature. Correctness does sometimes square with cost-control, however, a logic which says it is cheaper to shoot those two rebel scenes at once and trust that the intervening sunlight scene will not be particularly noticed.

That is one example of the drive for correctness behind the BBC production. There are others. The costume designer, Odette Barrow, did a great deal of research in order to give the production authentic dress. It is on record that the historical Hotspur incorporated his mother's coat of arms with his own after his mother died, for example. Here was an opportunity to get a detail exactly right. But it was found that Shakespeare destroyed this opportunity without realising it, by having the mother appear in *Part Two* (Lady Northumberland) after she should have been dead. Thus accuracy thwarts itself. If one cuts Lady Northumberland from *Part Two* in order to design the dead mother's arms on to Hotspur's shield in *Part One*, the authorial text has been violated just as badly as the authorial text itself violates historical accuracy by calling on Lady Northumberland after she should have been in the grave. Correctness is not easy.

The most useful piece of accuracy passed on by the BBC production concerns the King's illness, which Shakespeare never specifies. It was learned from the sources that this was leprosy, perhaps with a touch of syphilis, and that is why Jon Finch, as the King, is always rubbing his hands. This does add a dimension to the royal role if one catches on, but not everyone caught on in *Part One*, when the illness must have been in its earlier stages. 'Finch gives his king an embarrassing and irritating series of hand gestures as his sole means of displaying Henry's care, concern, guilt and insecurity,' wrote one reviewer. 'Finch cannot refrain, in his every scene, from indulging in the most amateurish sign language: he rubs his hands together, strokes the left with the right, plays nervously with his gloves and his signet ring, massages his forehead, and goes through

[103]

an elaborate ritual cleansing of those busy hands' (*Shakespeare on Film Newsletter*, quoted in Bulman and Coursen, p. 258).

The desire for the correct historical detail I take to be the same as the desire for the correct moral interpretation. To film a monument for all time puts up the pressure for accuracy. Such anxiety occupied the early efforts in the BBC project, and it was not until the series was well under way and Jonathan Miller became the producer that a spirit of experimentation with the medium of television itself became possible (Bulman, pp. 50-1). The most successful of the later productions reject the assumption that the viewer looks for naturalised spaces. Elijah Moshinsky's *All's Well That Ends Well* of 1981 turned the interiors into the kind of composed space found, for example, in Renaissance paintings (Hunter, p. 186). Jane Howell's history cycle of the *Henry VI* plays and *Richard III* of 1983 took place on a stage-set built of platforms, alcoves, and palisades. The camera had to move in accordance with these spaces (Bingham, pp. 221-9). In both cases, the camera became active and decisive in the visual compositions, the notion of realistic filming was left behind, and the viewer was challenged to keep track of things according to the angles and motions possible on spaces frankly made for television

But the BBC *1 Henry IV* came before these possibilities were being explored. Anthony Quayle's Falstaff is good to have. The jolt of his soliloquies, when he looks right in upon our privacy and breaks the code of realism by talking rascality to us, has the effect of interrupting the solemn, anxious, correct cycle meant for all time and reminding us that the decaying body and the quick wit can still join together for the sake of surviving even as history is being made. But the rest of the show is dull, and no one has paid it much heed, apart from schoolchildren who are assigned the opportunity to see their Shakespeare reading come to life on the little screen. As Maurice Charney said of the BBC history plays, 'everyone in these productions seems so concerned with the Cause of English History … that there is little room for David Gwillim [as Hal] to have any real fun that is not of an educationally preparative nature' (Charney, p. 289).

The Welles film and the BBC production make a useful pair for the contrast they provide – the contrast between the cultural imperialism of the BBC, filming a careful *1 Henry IV* to fill its niche in the complete works of Shakespeare for the ages to come, and the out-at-elbow improvisations of Welles, running all the Falstaff plays into one under the guise of doing *Treasure Island*. *Chimes at Midnight* has become an underground classic – hardly ever shown, but quite memorable to those who see it, and widely written about. The BBC tape, correct and dull, remains on the schoolroom shelf until the teacher assigns it. It is as difficult to dislike as it is difficult to view, and it makes no impact. Welles' film is underfunded, badly dubbed, never quite finished, disliked by Bosley Crowther of the *New York Times*, and permanently part of the the culture.

CHAPTER VII

1986. The English Shakespeare Company: Michael Bogdanov

In 1986 there opened a production of *1 Henry IV* that gave every impression of coming out of nowhere. Directed by Michael Bogdanov, the play began not with a guilt-ridden King complaining to his courtiers, 'So shaken as we are, so wan with care' (thus opening in a context of history), but with a company of actors in rehearsal clothes, some carrying their own musical instruments, coming on stage to sing a 'Ballad of Harry le Roy':

> Come all you good people, who would hear a song
> Of men brave and men bold, of men weak and men strong,
> Of a king who was mighty, but wild as a boy,
> And list to the ballad – of Harry le Roy.

The stage was cluttered with odd properties: an overstuffed pink chair, a dustbin with a folded blanket on it, a coat-rack with long khaki and tan overcoats hung from it, a microphone downstage centre. This was not 'history' or a 'stage-set'. This was a group of actors promising to make something out of the clutter. That is one phase of the 'out of nowhere' beginning. *

Another is that the singing actors had no previous existence as a company. This was the first play ever produced by this group. I have noted in earlier chapters how often *1 Henry IV* serves to mark a

---

*Production details are from the prompt-book of the original staging plus personal observation of the Toronto performances in the summer of 1987. I have checked my observations against extensive notes from the Toronto and Chicago performances kindly supplied by Barbara Hodgdon, who is writing on *2 Henry IV* for this series.

significant moment in a famous institution – the opening of the Old Vic's 1945 season, the Festival of Britain celebrations at Stratford, Shakespeare's birthday, the opening of the Barbican – but here there was no institution in the first place. Something called the 'English Shakespeare Company' was getting started here and now, a band of upstarts filling in the background of the play with their lilting, self-accompanied ballad, as though the text could not be counted on to do the job itself, and skewing the story a bit in the process:

> One year passes by, Henry Bolingbroke returns
> At the head of an army, for vengeance he burns,
> Defeats and imprisons King Richard alone,
> Then murders him shamefully, seizes the throne.

The most important thing the company lacked was a theatre of their own. Their productions were to be touring shows from the first, and before they finished they played over thirty cities in the United Kingdom, Europe, and Canada. To have a theatre of their own would have been an encumbrance, just as having a costume design would have been a encumbrance, or a permanent set, or even a fixed mailing address (which changed from Golden Square to Paddington Street to Duke Street to Sadlers Wells in the first three years). Their 'set' was really a 'kit' that could be trucked into a city and unpacked the night before the opening: a deep black box made of aluminum girders, with a bridge that could be flown, a scrim backdrop with sliding doors, and two trolley towers that could be rolled on-stage from each side. These people did not want to look like an institution. They wanted to look as if they had just come in from the street with an eye for this stage and these properties. From such things a play on Prince Hal and his father could be *constructed*, as it were.

Or so it seemed. Theatre is the art of illusion, and behind the impression of being unarranged lay many careful arrangements. *1 Henry IV* is the story of a prince who carefully plans the image of carelessness as a way of becoming great, and the actors who gave every impression of coming out of nowhere could not have been unaware that the hero of their first play gave the same impression by design. Prince Hal has far-reaching plans behind his apparent nonchalance, and when this new acting company came on the stage for the opening night of *1 Henry IV*, they were ready to open *2 Henry IV* and *Henry V* as well. They did not have a theatre of their own, but they did have a history cycle.

[107]

The director was Michael Bogdanov, and Hal was played by Michael Pennington. They had both done important work with the Royal Shakespeare Company and the National Theatre before founding this new company. Here is how Bogdanov describes the founding. There was no theatre, no money, no organisation. There were just Michael Bogdanov and Michael Pennington, the well-known director and the well-known actor, the 'two Michaels' as they came to be known in the company (once there was a company), having a coffee around the corner from 105 Picadilly. 105 Picadilly is the address of the Arts Council, and the two Michaels had just called in there with a notion of putting together a little touring group. The Arts Council had said we have plenty of little touring groups, what we want is something big, the two Michaels had gone around the corner to have a coffee, and there they said to themselves, why not do the two parts of *Henry IV* and *Henry V*? Then they went back to 105 Picadilly, and the Arts Council gave them £100,000.

That is how Bogdanov tells the story (quoted in Roberts, p. 20). Readers who have dealt with the Arts Council may wonder at the spontaneity with which these events are said to have happened, and there may be just a touch of Eastcheap joviality in the telling, as though the thought of doing three history plays pops into one's mind at the coffee shop as easily as doing a 'play extempore' does at the Boar's Head. This is not to suggest, of course, that there was any deliberate correspondence between the story of the origin of the English Shakespeare Company and the story of the origin of King Henry V which the company took as their first dramatic venture. These things happen naturally, like the sun coming out from behind the clouds, and if the story about the founding of the English Shakespeare Company has the quality of enduring legend about it, let the legend be told.

To name these actors the 'English Shakespeare Company' was itself an exercise in ambiguity. The name sounds something like the Royal Shakespeare Company, and its initials – the ESC – are identical to those of the English Stage Company, which made its reputation at the Royal Court in the 1960s. The new company was saying something about its parentage with its name, but what, exactly, was it saying? The child might be rebellious, the child might be dutiful, it is hard to be certain, as King Henry IV knew when he thought about *his* eldest son. The reviewers of *The Henrys*, as this cycle was called, were evenly divided on the question of

[108]

whether the new company was a threat to the Royal Shakespeare Company or a welcome addition to it, with conservative publications like the *The Financial Times* leaning towards the welcome addition and liberal ones like *City Limits* leaning towards the threat (*The Financial Times*, 26 March 1987, *City Limits*, 26 March 1987). Everyone agreed that the new company was doing something audacious in regard to the older one, an impression that continued as *The Henrys* were expanded a year later into a seven-play cycle on *The Wars of the Roses*, with marathon Saturdays when one could see plays morning, afternoon, and night. The Royal Shakespeare Company had made these devices of history-cycle and marathon days famous in 1964. They had even used the title, *The Wars of the Roses*. The audacity of the new company lay in so directly imitating the RSC without the permanent base of a theatre, a loyal audience, an ongoing subsidy, or even a mailing list at first.

By touring from the beginning, Bogdanov wanted to reach audiences new to Shakespeare, even audiences new to theatre itself. 'Basically my theatre – when I am working with Shakespeare – is designed for people who have never been to the theatre before' (Roberts, p. 21). Great Britain, he went on, consists of four or five nations – Northern Ireland, Scotland, Wales, the North-East, for example. London cultural rule tends to override these regional differences – 'a rule which of course in Henry V spreads to the annexation of a part of France'. By touring, presumably, Bogdanov meant to to acknowledge and dramatise the regional diversity that London culture overrides, and his production certainly made London rule in the person of Prince Hal/Henry V look overriding. Legend continues to operate here. The anti-intellectualism of Bogadanov's pose ('I have no time for those who already know the text backwards because they are the ones who finally kill off the theatre' – Roberts, p. 21) cannot disguise his company's dependence on the support of intellectuals wherever they go, and the challenge to 'London rule' is not quite fiery enough to lose contact with those sources of London capital and London publicity that the company needs. There is a certain regional panache in getting funds from the Allied Irish Bank and from Ed Mirvish of Toronto to go along with that grant from 105 Picadilly, but Commonwealth capitalists gravitate to London as normal business procedure. Ed Mirvish owns the Old Vic in London, where the company played its longest run, and the Allied Irish Bank was proud to receive a prize for 'Best Sponsorship Project' from a leading London newspaper.

[109]

The English Shakespeare Company may have had four office addresses, but they were all in central London.

This was a company that was trying to have it both ways – by challenging London cultural rule in their version of *The Henrys* on tour even as they counted on sources of London capital and prestige to keep their show on the road. The amazing thing is that they *succeeded* both ways, and the analogy to Prince Hal does not cease to be appropriate at this point. At the end of the 'Ballad of Henry le Roy,' before a line of Shakespeare's text had been spoken, the company cleared the stage of its properties while Michael Pennington as Hal stood a little to the side, watching them. Everyone knew this was Hal, although he was in rehearsal clothes like the others. Pennington had a wonderful knack of entering into things and keeping his distance from them at the same time. That was the mark of his Eastcheap scenes, and it was the way he joined the ballad at the beginning. He stood out even as he joined in, and one knew it was Hal. He was, of course, the subject they were singing about, but as he watched the others clear the stage, he looked as though he might also be the supervisor of the entire business. He was having it both ways too.

Prince Hal has it both ways by roistering in Eastcheap while he prepares to be King, Pennington both ways by joining the company while supervising it, Bogdanov both ways by telling of quick ideas over coffee while extending them into major financing for a seven-play cycle of history plays, the English Shakespeare Company both ways by acting like upstarts while imitating the Royal Shakespeare Company of twenty-five years before. Everything about this *1 Henry IV* had an aura of doubleness about it, a consistency of contradiction from the inner fiction of Hal's story to the outer legend of the company's origin. Theatre is the art of contradiction, of making people see the illusory as the real, and in the ESC's first production that art was displayed from the surface to the core.

* * *

The one member of the company not on stage for the opening ballad was John Woodvine. He was playing Falstaff, and as he was already padded and made-up backstage, he could not fit into the 'rehearsal-clothes' device of the song. He was already in costume, and this Falstaff's costumes were the most outlandish on record: a green velvet smoking-jacket with checked trousers that might have belonged in a circus, a 1940s double-breasted George Melly suit, a feathered Australian hat to go with an Army poncho in the robbery scene. He was an aristocrat absolutely confident in his own bad taste, and as he amounted to a theatre in himself, he could not very well join the unconstructed theatre of the opening.

Woodvine had played Falstaff before, for a Royal Shakespeare Company production of *The Merry Wives of Windsor* in 1979-80. His performance then was notable for its realism rather than its buffoonery, and he reminded several reviewers of down-and-out old military officers or gentlemen gone to seed whom they had observed in bars or at the track (reviews quoted in Trussler, *1979/80*, p. 9). Part of the excitement of the ESC production was seeing this pressure towards realism, which is Woodvine's strong tendency, turned towards the iconoclasm and overt theatricality of Bogdanov's style. Different artistic temperaments were having to give and take, and the result was riveting. This was a Falstaff aimed towards psychological credibility in a production that often seemed to disrupt such consistency of intention – and it used to be the other way around. Falstaff, it used to be thought, disrupted a regime that was striving for credibility. Now he was trying to make sense in a world which could not even settle into one period. The costuming around him ranged from medieval chain-mail through Victorian morning-coats to contemporary punk. Through it all, Woodvine's Falstaff was, of all things, a centre of stability, a classical performance visible through those outlandish costumes, a figure one could almost count on in the midst of the image-breaking around him.

The result was a wonderful performance. The critics (who were not of one voice about the overall production) all thought Woodvine's Falstaff was superb. In a *1 Henry IV* intended to be anti-heroic, Woodvine received the 1987 Laurence Olivier Award for Best Comedy Performance. The *Manchester Evening News* voted him Best Actor in a Visiting Production. 'A creation of such epic proportions that I expect to take it with me to my grave', said *Punch* (8 April 1987); 'a beautifully articulated reading', said *The Financial Times* (March 1987); 'a hundred good moments in his performance', said the *Guardian* (23 March 1987); 'not since Ralph Richardson played the role can lovableness and roguery have been more adroitly balanced', said the *Sunday Telegraph* (29 March 1987).

The comparison to Richardson was made often. It was meant to give Woodvine credit, but I am not certain it did justice to his performance. Woodvine was not playing Falstaff for the lovable and pathetic roguery that Richardson drew so memorably from the part. Woodvine's Falstaff was dangerous, not lovable, and he was dangerous for two reasons that set him apart from Richardson. One is technical, a matter of the voice. Richardson's voice was one of his limitations as an actor. His projection was exceptional, but what he projected was a dry voice that reminded some listeners of sandpaper. Woodvine has one of the most penetrating bass-baritones of the English theatre, an instrument of great intelligibility that can rattle the fixtures at the rear of the stalls without losing a word. His Falstaff was fond of turning this voice into a higher-pitched nasal drawl, a sneer from some decayed aristocratic source aimed at a target that could not quite be fixed. The danger came from the uncertainty of the target. Anyone could be the victim of this mimicry, which could arise just when one was being tempted to think this rogue lovable and Ralph Richardson all over again.

The other element of danger was Falstaff's sense of his own worth. Richardson emphasised the broken-hearted moments – not just the moment of rejection by Hal in *Part Two*, but also the moments when an awareness of death cannot be jollied away. It was a great sentimental reading, but sentiment is just what Woodvine avoided. His Falstaff was looking for recognition on the assumption that he deserved it. The soliloquy on 'honour' was not a comic monologue. Woodvine took honour to be a crucial dilemma for Falstaff, who would like to believe that he had once possessed it himself and who could see himself as superior to the *other* aristocrats, for they were bum-suckers and liars. It did not matter that Falstaff was wrong about much of this (although right about some of the other aristocrats). His self-delusion was driven by substantial motives, and one who found this man 'lovable' was likely to pay for the error in the long run.

His conclusion in the soliloquy – that honour is useless because 'detraction will not suffer it' (V. ii. 138) – reminded one that this Falstaff has always been sensitive about his dismal reputation and prone to moments of self-annoyance about his cravings for alcohol and food. To be annoyed with himself on that score was part of the realism of Woodvine's interpretation. But this Falstaff also ate and drank more than any within memory, and some of the gluttony looked less like realism, more like a Bogdanov gag. 'Bardolph, am I not fallen away vilely since this last action?' at the start of III. iii was introduced by the wonderful business of Falstaff's cracking six eggs into a mug, sloshing in a dose of gin, and drinking the concoction straight off, while Bardolph, seated at the same table, played a lugubrious 'Darling, I am growing older' on his slide trombone. A moment later Falstaff was calling for his breakfast. But his vow to repent and spend more time in church had a touch of desolation, as though Falstaff could become disgusted with himself if only the temptations of the flesh (and the gags of a good director) would leave him alone for a moment longer. Honour was certainly a lost cause for this reprobate, but he could regret the loss in little bursts of self-annoyance.

We all appreciate an actor's realism, but do we appreciate gags? Some of the reviewers were troubled by what they regarded as the 'childishness' of using the eclectic costuming to introduce gratuitous contemporary props and tricks. While the royal forces at Shrewsbury were mainly decked in bright red cavalry outfits, and Hal wore medieval chain-mail, Falstaff – glancing right and left, always ready to hide or collapse in a heap – wore twentieth-century camouflage fatigues. This led to a gag when Douglas drew his sword furiously across Falstaff's belly during their encounter at the Battle of Shrewsbury. It looked as though Falstaff must really be wounded. How could light military fabric protect all that flesh from the blade? But then Falstaff pulled a 'no-entry' traffic sign out from under his uniform – Douglas's thrust had landed there. Such gags were always threatening to break out, and some of us in the audience saw jokes that the actors did not even know about. In the tavern scene, when Falstaff said 'There be four of us here have ta'en a thousand pound' (II. iv. 152), the tavern crowd all stopped their conversations and turned to listen intently. Americans in the audience recognised an allusion to an often-repeated television commercial which showed everyone turning to listen when a rich man mentioned the name of his broker: 'when E. F. Hutton talks, everybody listens'. But none of the cast had ever seen the E. F. Hutton commercial when they were asked about this later. True gags are in the mind of the beholder. In *Part Two*, Pistol arrived at Justice Shallow's orchard by motor cycle, and his jacket was emblazoned 'Hal's Angels'. That one must have been intended, and those in the audience who take their Shakespeare pure were distressed by such moments. But the gags were signs of an underlying seriousness, a tough determination to keep the production open to the unexpected and to demand that the audience remain uncertain of what might happen next.

[113]

The key scene for Woodvine's interpretation was V.iv, where Falstaff pretends to have killed Hotspur himself. Shakespeare makes this a private piece of rascality which Hal tolerates as another example that Falstaff is 'the strangest fellow'. Well into the rehearsal period, Bogdanov (taking a lead from *Chimes at Midnight*) thought of deferring Falstaff's entrance with the corpse of Hotspur until the next scene, when his claim to have won the heroic combat himself would be public and even made before the King himself. With a cut at the end of V.iv, Falstaff would exit with the corpse of Percy before Hal discovered what the rascal was up to. Moving directly to V. v would bring Hal and his father on stage, and they would be surprised to see Falstaff enter with the corpse, bringing the end of the previous scene with him as a sort of coda. It would be in front of the King himself that Falstaff would say: 'If your father will do me any honour, so; if not, let him kill the next Percy himself. I look to be either earl or duke, I can assure you' (V. iv. 137-9). This would be aggressively self-assertive but it would also do considerable damage to Hal, turning his claim to have killed Percy himself into a lie.

Woodvine took a while to accustom himself to this change (as he told me in an interview), but in the end he seized it as a moment of *hubris* that would bring to a climax Falstaff's distorted concern for honour. He could now claim renown for being the hero of Shrewsbury (the Coleville scene in *Part Two* falls more easily into place), and Hal's need to prove himself to his father a second time clearly follows. Pennington's Hal was furious at the humiliation before his father, and the resulting estrangement between him and Falstaff became the mark of their relationship in *Part Two*, where they have only one scene together before the final repudiation. Thus the change satisfied Woodvine's interest in credible characterisation and Bogdanov's penchant for driving the text new ways.

How this Falstaff could be seen as lovable and Richardsonian is hard to fathom. At any rate, Prince Hal did not love this Falstaff, that much is certain. This Hal did not love anybody (certainly not himself). He used Falstaff for his own interests from time to time, even cuddling up to him in one early scene – a hint of Alan Howard's 1975 RSC portrayal of a Hal who needed physical affection – but this was a rare sign in a Hal who hardly ever touched anyone.

Most of all, he avoided touching his father. This was the bleakest father–son relationship in modern productions, outdoing even the

Alan Howard–Emrys James version, and in this case the misunderstanding was fully evident on both sides. Patrick O'Connell's King, absorbed with political image-making, had no sensitivity for the young: everyone should act grown-up and get on with the job. There was more than a hint of Mrs Thatcher here. The leading idea of the production was that the refusal of communication between this repressive father and the anxiety-ridden son he produced would have political consequences – fatal for many – in the kingdom and overseas. The Falklands War was recent history when this production took shape, and some early rehearsals were held at the Mountbatten RAF base near Plymouth, where real troopers in camouflage – minor imitations of Falstaff – were preparing for war rehearsals in the Channel (Ackerman, p. 64). Anti-imperialism was a strong and consistent theme in this version of Hal's 'development' into the warrior-King of Agincourt.

The interview scene between father and son was a study of unpredictability. Hal's first response to his father's rebuke, a speech in which he is supposed to 'beg' extenuation, was delivered as a mock set-piece, the sort of cynicism with which he has been driving his father wild for years. Probably the father has replied with the same lecture before: you are just like Richard II, you mingle too easily with popularity, you don't know how to stage yourself sparingly as a King must do. On and on he went in this vein, and Pennington's Hal was ready to twiddle his thumbs. He knew all about staging himself – his first soliloquy was an essay in how he would stage himself when the time was right – and the lecture he was hearing was really a demonstration of how little the father knew his son.

But something snapped in Hal when the King compared him to Hotspur. This is where the battle will really be fought, Hal thought – the battle for his father's admiration as well as the battle for his own authority – and Pennington opened himself to his father in a fury, vowing to 'tear the reckoning' from Percy's heart (III. ii. 152). That Hal could reveal himself to his father only in terms of violence seemed true and frightening. The hero of Agincourt was making himself apparent, his future greatness taking shape here in the anger of a son whose father does not know him, and a son who lacks the maturity to let himself be known.

From here it would have been easy to end the interview on a note of reconciliation, but this production rarely settled for something easy. The text makes it look as though the father and son are in harmony, as they exchange hyperboles:

> *Hal.* And I will die a hundred thousand deaths
> Ere break the smallest parcel of this vow.
> *King.* A hundred thousand rebels die in this! (III. ii. 158-60)

But Pennington rejected the King's embrace on 'a hundred thousand rebels', as though he could not let his father close the circle. They were no closer at the end than at the beginning of this brilliant, unsettling scene. How little Hal would give to this rigid father was stunningly clear, as was the violence that would erupt in the kingdom from their refusal to understand each other.

* * *

Part of the shock of this encounter was Hal's costume, for to this interview with his Victorian-clad father he wore torn blue jeans. This father and son were so far out of touch they came from different periods. But a mixture of period styles ran through the entire production. Bogdanov's trademark is Shakespeare in modern dress, but even he thought the single combat between Hal and Hotspur at Shrewsbury required armour and swords. Rather than give in to period costuming throughout, Bogdanov and his costumer Stephanie Howard held back on their decisions and let the actors have something to say as they worked into their roles. Most productions begin with the actors looking at costume designs which have already been laid out for them, but in this case the costume decisions were left open while the company spent their early rehearsals listening to Bogdanov talk about Shakespeare and history, then 'putting the scenes on the floor' to see how they might look. The intention was to observe the images given off by the actors as they rehearsed and to let the costuming reflect those images. Pennington himself felt that denim and hiking boots were right for Hal in the Eastcheap scenes (he told me in an interview). This would set the Prince's adolescence apart from the punk and leather attitudes of the other young people there. It would also, Pennington said, reflect something of his own observations of adolescence. Blue jeans on the Prince of Wales were one of the images the critics found shocking, but there is no doubt that holding costume decisions open until well along in rehearsals helped create the charged immediacy of Pennington's performance.

Bogdanov and Stephanie Howard gradually worked out visual

ideas for each group: the northern rebels wore bits and pieces picked from the rail, in a 'pot-pourri of rebellion through the ages' (Stephanie Howard's phrase, in an interview with me), while the King and courtiers needed something more consistent, as befits power on display. Bogdanov favoured modern business suits at first, as part of his career-long campaign to stereotype the bureaucrat, but Stephanie Howard and the actors wanted formal dress from the past, and it was finally agreed to use Victorian frock-coats and scarlet tunics as a way of giving a 'layering' of period to the power image. The decision was important. It broadened the reference to power, for these ministers of state in the opening scene, for example, looked like Victorians while using the media technology of today (the microphone) to present what were, after all, fifteenth-century political references. This took the 'heart' out of the King's opening complaint in 'So shaken as we are ...' and supplied a political point instead. His confessional mode on guilt and the hope for repentance now became a media presentation: Henry IV and Richard Nixon had something in common, and they looked like Gladstone. *

The different periods of dress offended those who favour proper history. Giles Gordon complained that 'the crucial hierarchical distinctions of fifteenth century England go for nothing' (*London Daily News*, 23 March 1987), Michael Billington found the effect 'reductive and confusing' (*Guardian*, 23 March 1987), and Irving Wardle thought the sense of history had been lost (*The Times*, 23 March 1987). Even those who praised the production wondered at the 'anything goes' spirit, with Robin Ray comparing Bogdanov to 'a berserk chef' whipping up a stir-fry and 'using anything and everything available' (*Punch*, 8 April 1987). One of the intentions of the production was liable to be lost in such complaints, for the costuming at its best was more than a *mélange* and did have a logic to it.

Take the tavern scenes, for example. Everyone saw the modern costuming: Hal in blue jeans danced with a punked-up Doll

---

*Making the King's opening speech into a press-conference had been done in a modern-dress production at Santa Cruz, California, in 1984. For a full account of this version, which in some ways anticipated the ESC, see Dunbar, pp. 475-6, and Dessen, pp. 71-9. Costuming from various periods was used in Joan Littlewood's production for the Edinburgh Festival in 1964 and in the Indiana Repertory Theatre's production at Indianapolis in 1984.

Tearsheet (Jenny Quayle in black leather bustier, mini-skirt, torn fishnet tights, and ankle boots). The on-stage band, 'Sneak's Noise', was amplified. But the drawers and background customers were out of the nineteenth century: waistcoats, britches, long dresses. If Hal and Doll were rocking in an East End pub of today, the others were Dickensian. Falstaff, in his outrageously loud checked trousers, was in a world of his own. Where was this tavern? When? There was no way to answer those questions, but the consistency within the layers and the contrast between them – the punk layer set against the nineteenth-century layer – made the questions impossible to disregard. This was not an 'anything goes' timelessness. It was instead an England of partial consistencies, the elements refusing to fit with one another but refusing to collapse into randomness either. Hal's job would be to whip this diversity into a shape of his own design as the cycle of plays progressed; but here in the tavern scenes, while he was still looking for opportunities and finding his way, something valuable was on display. This variegated England was not polite, and certainly not wealthy, but it was, of all things, when one stopped to consider it, civilised.

Of course Hal paused in the middle of 'I do, I will.' He was not discovering something spontaneously, as Richard Burton had done. He had seen the opportunity coming, had planned it a little ahead: a chance to practise the role he would later take on. This Hal could freeze the heart at moments, and if it is accurate to call the layered tavern scenes 'civilised' even with their disreputability and unruliness, one also has to admit that the Hal who can reject what he does not find useful and force the rest into an instrument of overseas destruction is despicable. The taunting of Francis, the drawer, illustrates the point. Hal was a little drunk by this time, and was being utterly malicious. Even Poins thought this joke pointless. But John Tramper's delicately etched Francis loved the Prince no matter what games were being played. His 'anon, anon' to Poins was not the cry of a servant torn in two directions, but the acknowledgment of a small nuisance named Poins off to the side. Who is this man to be bothering me – the Prince is here! Francis was magnetised by Hal even as he was being manipulated. This kind of allegiance can be beneficial if the authority be sound and confident, but Hal had to twist it to his own neurotic ends, building it through jingoism and manipulation into the psychology of mob-hooliganism that would eventually produce victory at Agincourt. In *Henry V* the actor of Francis played the Boy killed at Agincourt, and

[118]

the visual reminder was unmistakable.

That is what eventually happened. But in the tavern scenes the ruthless Hal was only momentarily apparent. He had his civilised side too. To protect Falstaff from the authorities who enter at the end of the first tavern scene, Hal summoned an astonishing Gadshill to play a Mozartian tune on his flute. Gadshill had his head shaved bald, except for an enormous Mohican plume that arose from his skull. He was aggressively punk – strong men would cross the King's Road to avoid him. (The same actor, Andrew Jarvis, would play Richard III when the cycle was complete.) But in the world of this tavern, he could improvise ravishing melodies on his flute. When the Lord Chief Justice himself came after Falstaff (there was no Sheriff in this production, and the Chief Justice's role in *Part Two* was being established here), he was confronted by a Prince tipped back in his chair, eyes closed in rapture, waving his finger in accompaniment to a classical flute played by a Mohawked punk bully-boy in a tavern that might have been in Eastcheap, Dickens, or Stepney-heath. There was nothing a Chief Justice could do in such circumstances. He just stood there. Power cannot gain a foothold in the face of such incongruity. To make power wait until the comedy and the beauty are played out is what I mean by calling the tavern scenes 'civilised,' and the Hal who had just chilled everyone with his treatment of Francis and his 'I do, I will' to Falstaff now looked like he had humorous and humane possibilities after all.

* * *

Hotspur appears in II. iv reading a letter about the rebellion. Olivier, standing with one foot on the ground, the other on a chair, so that his doublet was riding high and his tight-fitted legs could be seen, played this moment for its statuesque effect. Who has ever read a letter with one foot on a chair? But he looked good, especially in his neatly trimmed ginger beard. In Bogdanov's production John Price read the letter stripped to the waist, shaving, his face covered with lather. Not many letters have been read that way either, but shaving put Hotspur into motion from the beginning, and in motion he remained. Price was a vibrant, physical Hotspur, full of energy and a bit thick, the sort who might actually dive in and try to pluck up drowned honour by the locks. Only one person was a physical match for him, and that was Lady Percy (played with marvellous energy by Jennie Stoller). Their 'argument' scene was a rough-and-tumble delight. Against this roistering Hotspur, however, it was clear that Pennington's Hal, cringing from physical contact, would not stand up in single combat.

Indeed, when it came to single combat at the Battle of Shrewsbury, Hotspur had the fight won. Pennington played the only Hal who actually lost the single combat. Hotspur was stronger and more of a fighter. He knocked the sword and shield out of Hal's hands and forced him to his knees. It was all over for the Prince of Wales, who was cowering and praying to some unknown deity, waiting for the fatal blow to strike from behind. He was saved by his opponent's chivalry – Hotspur would not kill an unarmed man. There was no trace of Merrie-England nostalgia about this chivalry. It was a code of honour long past its prime and vulnerable to the political manipulations of the other rebel leaders (Worcester and Northumberland could get Hotspur to do anything they wanted by heating his blood over a question of honour). Now, with Hal down and helpless in the single combat, chivalry intervened as a piece of stupidity. Hotspur bent over to slide Hal's sword back to him, and within an instant Hal was driving that sword into him from behind.

This was the moment the 1945 Old Vic production had immortalised when Hal completed Hotspur's stutter on 'worms'. Pennington's Hal had no interest in such formality. He stole the line away from Hotspur as he again drove his sword into the back of his enemy's neck. This was the Hal who vowed he would 'tear the reckoning' from Hotspur's heart, and he was being true to his promise. What that truth indicated for England, however, was hard to name. Hotspur's code of chivalry, outdated though it was, at least had recognisable standards of behaviour, but Hal's victory asserted nothing but his own determination to gain credit before a society and a father who refused to take him as seriously as he took himself. So, with luck, he used violence to establish his credibility, and it did not work. Hal was staging himself without an audience, and his violence looked like a back-alley killing. That oddly private part of the battlefield where Shakespeare sets the single combat could now be understood. Virtually no one sees the single combat in which Hal thinks to emerge a hero. The unseen theatrical performance is superfluous, as Falstaff knows. Nothing *remains* superfluous in the presence of Falstaff (his huge girth is a metaphor of that), and as John Woodvine stole the corpse away then returned with it in the next scene when an audience was available, to present 'his' prize before the King, one realised that Hal – having rubbed out the system of chivalry in killing Hotspur – was now being outdone by the system that has taken over in modern politics, the system of theatrical publicity.

Hal was left virtually alone at the end of this production. His father had stalked away thinking him a liar, Falstaff had walked off with the honours of Shrewsbury, his brother (Prince John) had seized the opportunity to sneer at him once more, and that sneer represented the attitude of the ruling class whose leader he was supposed to become. As Hal exited alone, he raised his sword over his head in an odd gesture of bitterness. The same gesture had been made earlier by a character with whom Hal should have little in common – the rebel Douglas. Douglas is no future king. The bald Andrew Jarvis played him as the last Scotsman on the face of the earth, kilted and stripped to the waist, overcoming his vulnerability by sheer fury. He would raise his swords (for he fought with two swords and no shield) over his head in a sort of Highlands Kung Fu gesture of individualism. Douglas had no father, no family, no crown to strive for, no commitment beyond the combat of the moment. For Hal to reflect Douglas for a second was a sign of his isolation and the futility of his design for heroism. No future King was evident at the end of *Part One*.

As Hal exited, a figure stood to the side of the stage, playing a mournful melody on a flute. It was, of all people, Douglas. Or, to put it more exactly, it was Andrew Jarvis still dressed as Douglas, the Andrew Jarvis who appeared in various roles when flute music was needed. He had been Gadshill, outrageously punked, playing the flute in the tavern scene, and he had been one of the Welsh musicians at Glendower's castle. His flute music was always quiet and mournful, in contrast to the amplified Christian chorales and fugues sponsored by the royal family. The flute was the sound of societies being wiped out by the dynasty – the Eastcheap world, the Welsh world, the Douglas world, rebels all of them, and unlike the royal family capable of hearing something subtle and natural – ragtag people, capable of violence but also capable of preserving the culture. This final image of Hal's isolated exit with the flute heard off to the side suggested the thoughtful care that lay behind this production. Hal's gesture made one think of Douglas and his simple fury, a sign of adolescent failure, but Douglas himself was standing to the side, without a sword now, playing a flute, the flute being played by the actor who had threaded his sad music through Eastcheap, Wales, and now Shrewsbury, the music of a rebellion that had the remnants of real culture within it. This is what Hal had to destroy. Not that it was particularly worth saving. The Eastcheap people were crooked, the Welsh unreliable, the Percies a bit stupid. Flute melodies can only go so far in building a culture. As I have mentioned, this production ruled out the sentimental possibilities. Its combination of iconoclasm and intelligence provided something that sentimentality can never approach, however – an opportunity to think beyond the staged moment to other parts of the production, and beyond those to other royal families, other rebellions, other authorities whose power is based on insecurity and the use of force. By refusing to dress 'England' in any one period, Bogdanov and the company portrayed a nation whose variegation was still distinct but threatened by the establishment of a centralised government with no strength beyond publicity and violence. That this government arose in the fifteenth century was no more certain than that it was arising today – and both possibilities were certain enough to dislodge the Shakespeare history plays from the national pride they often serve and make them a source of watchful anger instead.

BIBLIOGRAPHY

Ackerman, Marianne, 'Mirvish, Marx, and Shakespeare', *Canadian Theatre Review*, 50, l987, 62-5.

Addenbrooke, David, *The Royal Shakespeare Company: The Peter Hall Years*, London, 1974.

Andrew, Dudley, *Film in the Aura of Art*, Princeton, 1984.

Barton, John, *Playing Shakespeare*, London, 1984.

Beauman, Sally (ed.), *The Royal Shakespeare Company's Production of Henry V*, Oxford, 1976.

—, *The Royal Shakespeare Company*, Oxford, 1982.

Bevington, David (ed.), *Henry IV, Part One*, Oxford, 1987.

Bingham, Dennis, 'Jane Howell's First Tetralogy: Brechtian Break-Out or Just Good Television?', in *Shakespeare on Television*, ed. Bulman and Coursen, Hanover, NH, 1988, pp. 221-9.

Bragg, Melvyn, *Richard Burton: A Life*, Boston, 1988.

Brown, John Russell, *Shakespeare in Performance: an Introduction Through Six Major Plays*, New York, 1973.

Bulman, J. C., 'The BBC Shakespeare and "House Style"', in *Shakespeare on Television*, ed. Bulman and Coursen, Hanover, NH, 1988, pp. 50-60.

—, and Coursen, H. R. (eds.), *Shakespeare on Television: An Anthology of Essays and Reviews*, Hanover, NH, 1988.

Burton, Hal, *Great Acting*, New York, 1967.

Charney, Maurice, 'Shakespearean Anglophilia: The BBC-TV Series and American Audiences', *Shakespeare Quarterly*, 31, 1980, 287-92.

Cottrell, John, and Cashin, Fergus, *Richard Burton: A Biography*, London, 1971.

David, Richard, 'Shakespeare's History Plays: Epic or Drama?', *Shakespeare Survey*, 6, 1953, 129-39.

—, *Shakespeare in the Theatre*, Cambridge, 1978.

Dent, Edward J., *A Theatre for Everybody: The Story of The Old Vic and Sadler's Wells*, London, 1945.

Dessen, Alan, 'Staging Shakespeare's History Plays in 1984: a Tale of Three Henrys', *Shakespeare Quarterly*, 36 ,1985, 71-9.

Dollimore, Jonathan, and Sinfield, Alan, *Political Shakespeare*, Manchester University Press, 1985.

Dunbar, Mary Judith, '*Henry IV* and *The Tempest* at Santa Cruz', *Shakespeare Quarterly*, 35, 1984, 475-6.

Elsom, John, and Tomalin, Nicholas, *The History of the National Theatre*,

London, 1978.

Evans, Gareth Lloyd, 'The Twentieth Century and "Behaviourism"', *Shakespeare Survey*, 20, l967, 133-42.

—, 'The Reason Why: The Royal Shakespeare Season 1968 Reviewed', *Shakespeare Survey*, 22, 1969, 135-44.

Findlater, Richard, *Michael Redgrave: Actor*, London, 1956.

—, *These Our Actors*, London, 1983.

Hapgood, Robert, 'Chimes at Midnight: The Art of Adaptation', *Shakespeare Survey*, 39, 1986, 39-52.

Hemingway, Samuel B., *New Variorum Edition of Henry IV, Part I*, Philadelphia, 1936.

Henry IV, Part I: The BBC TV Shakespeare, London, 1979.

Horovitz, Israel, *Henry Lumper*, New York, l990.

Hunter, G. K., 'The BBC *All's Well That Ends Well*', in *Shakespeare on Television*, ed. Bulman and Coursen, Hanover, NH, 1988, pp. 185-7.

Jorgens, Jack, *Shakespeare on Film*, Bloomington, Indiana, 1977.

Leiter, Samuel L. (ed.), *Shakespeare around the Globe: a Guide to Notable Postwar Revivals*, New York, 1986.

Lyons, Bridget Gellert and Dorothy Remy (eds.), *Chimes at Midnight, Orson Welles, director*, New Brunswick, 1988.

McMillin, Scott, 'The Moon in the Morning and the Sun at Night: Perversity and the BBC Shakespeare', in *Shakespeare on Television*, ed. Bulman and Coursen, Hanover, NH, 1988, pp. 76-81.

Morgann, Maurice, *Essay on the Dramatic Character of Sir John Falstaff*, London, 1777.

Mullin, Michael, 'Emrys James: On Playing Henry IV', *Theatre Quarterly*, 7, 1977, 15-23.

O'Conner, Garry, *Ralph Richardson: An Actor's Life*, revised edition, London, 1986.

Odell, George C. D., *Shakespeare from Betterton to Irving*, 2 vols., New York, 1966.

Olivier, Laurence, *On Acting*, New York, 1986.

Redgrave, Michael, *The Actor's Ways and Means*, New York, 1953.

Roberts, Peter, 'Shakespeare Our Contemporary', *Plays International*, October l986.

Sales, Roger (ed.), *Shakespeare in Perspective*, vol. l, London, 1982.

Sarlos, Robert K., 'Dinglestadt's Celebration of the Tercentenary: Shakespeare's Histories as a Cycle', *Theatre Survey*, 5, 1964, 117-31.

Speaight, Robert, 'Shakespeare in Britain', *Shakespeare Quarterly*, 15, 1964, 377-89.

—, *Shakespeare on the Stage*, London, 1973.

—, 'Shakespeare in Britain,' *Shakespeare Quarterly*, 26, 1975, 15-23.

Sprague, Arthur Colby, *Shakespearean Players and Performances*, Cambridge, MA, 1953.

—, *Shakespeare's Histories: Plays for the Stage*, London, 1964.

—, and Trewin, J. C., *Shakespeare's Plays Today*, London, 1970.

Styan, J. L., *Shakespeare's Stagecraft*, Cambridge, 1967.

Thomson, Peter, 'Towards a Poor Shakespeare: The Royal Shakespeare Company at Stratford in 1975', *Shakespeare Survey*, 29, l976, 151-6.

Tillyard, E. M. W., *Shakespeare's History Plays*, London, 1944.

Trussler, Simon (ed.), *The Royal Shakespeare Company, 1979/80*, London, 1979.

—, (ed.), *The Royal Shakespeare Company, 1980/81*, Stratford, 1982.

—, (ed.), *The Royal Shakespeare Company, 1982/83*, Stratford, 1983.

Trewin, J. C., *Shakespeare on the English Stage*, London, 1964.

Tynan, Kenneth, *Showpeople: Profiles in Entertainment*, New York, 1970.

Waldock, A. J. A., 'Men in Buckram', *Review of English Studies*, old series, 23, 1947, 16-23.

Waller, Gary F., 'Decentering the Bard: The BBC-TV Shakespeare and Some Implications for Criticism and Teaching', in *Shakespeare on Television*, ed. Bulman and Coursen, Hanover, NH, 1988, pp. 18-30.

Wharton, T. F., *Text and Performance: Henry the Fourth, Parts 1 and 2*, London, 1983.

Williams, Harcourt, *Old Vic Saga*, London, 1949.

Williams, Simon, *Shakespeare on the German Stage*, vol. 1, Cambridge, 1990.

Williamson, Audrey, *Old Vic Drama*, London, 1948.

Wilson, J. Dover, *The Fortunes of Falstaff*, Cambridge, 1945.

—, and Worsley, T. C., *Shakespeare's Histories at Stratford, 1951*, New York, 1952.

APPENDIX

A. Significant twentieth-century productions of *1 Henry IV*

1906	Frank Benson	Stratford-upon-Avon
1921	Barry Jackson	Birmingham
1945	John Burrell	Old Vic
1951	Anthony Quayle	Stratford-upon-Avon
1955	Douglas Seale	Old Vic
1957	Roger Planchon	Villeurbanne and Paris
1958	Michael Langham	Stratford, Ontario
1964	Peter Hall	Stratford-upon-Avon
1966	Orson Welles	Locations in Spain (film)
1975	Terry Hands	Stratford-upon-Avon
1979	Peter Moss	Stratford, Ontario
1979	David Giles	BBC Television
1982	Trevor Nunn	Stratford-upon-Avon
1984	Ariane Mnouchkine	Paris
1984	Michael Edwards	Santa Cruz, California
1986	Michael Bogdanov	Plymouth and on tour

B. Adaptation

1985 Israel Horovitz, *Henry Lumper.* Gloucester Stage Company, Gloucester, Mass. Modernised and Americanised version of *1* and *2 Henry IV*, with the struggle between the rebellious Percys and the ruling 'Boleys' (cf. Bolingbroke) taking place in a waterfront labour union in a fishing town very like Gloucester, Mass. Text available (see Bibliography).

C. Major actors and production staff in productions described.

Old Vic, 1945
Director: John Burrell Costumes: Roger Furse
Scenery: Gower Parks Music: Gordon Menges

Henry IV Nicholas Hannen		*Mortimer* David Kentish
Prince Hal Michael Warre		*Glendower* Harcourt Williams
Falstaff Ralph Richardson		*Bardolph* Michael Raghan
Hotspur Laurence Olivier		*Mistress Quickly* Sybil Thorndike
Worcester George Relph		*Lady Percy* Margaret Leighton
Northumberland Miles Malleson		*Lady Mortimer* Diana Maddox

Stratford-upon-Avon, 1951

Director: Anthony Quayle Design: Tanya Moiseiwitsch,
with John Kidd   with Alix Stone
Music: Leslie Bridgewater

Henry IV Harry Andrews	*Mortimer* Peter Williams
Prince Hal Richard Burton	*Glendower* Hugh Griffith
Falstaff Anthony Quayle	*Bardolph* Michael Bates
Hotspur Michael Redgrave	*Mistress Quickly* Rosalind Atkinson
Worcester Duncan Lamont	*Lady Percy* Barbara Jefford
Northumberland Alexander Gauge	*Lady Mortimer* Sybil Williams

Stratford-upon-Avon, 1964

Director: Peter Hall, with John Barton and Clifford Williams
Design: John Bury Music: Guy Woolfenden

Henry IV Eric Porter	*Glendower* William Squire
Prince Hal Ian Holm	*Bardolph* John Normington
Falstaff Hugh Griffith	*Mistress Quickly* Patience Collier
Hotspur Roy Dotrice	*Lady Percy* Janet Suzman
Worcester Clive Morton	*Lady Mortimer* Katherine Barker
Northumberland David Waller	

Chimes at Midnight (film), 1966

Director: Orson Welles Costumes: Orson Welles
Photography: Edmond Richard Music: Angelo Francesco Lavagnino

Henry IV John Gielgud	*Bardolph* Paddy Bedford
Prince Hal Keith Baxter	*Mistress Quickly* Margaret Rutherford
Falstaff Orson Welles	
Hotspur Norman Rodway	*Doll Tearsheet* Jeanne Moreau
Worcester Fernando Rey	*Lady Percy* Marina Vlady
Northumberland Jose Nieto	

Stratford-upon-Avon, 1975

Director: Terry Hands Designer: Farrah

Henry IV Emrys James	*Glendower* Griffith Jones
Prince Hal Alan Howard	*Bardolph* Tim Wylton
Falstaff Brewster Mason	*Mistress Quickly* Maureen Pryor
Hotspur Stuart Wilson	*Lady Percy* Ann Hasson
Northumberland Clement McCallin	*Lady Mortimer* Yvonne Nicholson

BBC Television, 1979

Director: David Giles Designer: Don Homfrey
Costumes: Odette Barrow

Henry IV Jon Finch	*Hotspur* Tim Pigott-Smith
Prince Hal David Gwillim	*Worcester* Clive Swift
Falstaff Anthony Quayle	*Northumberland* Bruce Purchase

[127]

Mortimer Robert Morris *Lady Percy* Michele Dotrice
Bardolph Gordon Gostelow *Lady Mortimer* Sharon Morgan
Mistress Quickly Brenda Bruce

English Shakespeare Company, 1986
Director: Michael Bogdanov Costumes: Stephanie Howard
Set Design: Chris Dyer Music: Terry Mortimer
Henry IV Patrick O'Connell *Glendower* Gareth Thomas
Prince Hal Michael Pennington *Douglas* Andrew Jarvis
Falstaff John Woodvine *Bardolph* Colin Farrell
Hotspur John Price *Mistress Quickly* June Watson
Northumberland Hugh Sullivan *Lady Percy* Jennie Stoller
Worcester Donald Gee *Lady Mortimer* Eluned Hawkins
Mortimer Charles Dale

INDEX

[132]